MILITARY MAYHEM

MILITARY MAYHEM

edited by
Raymond Horricks

British Library Cataloguing in Publication Data
Horricks, Raymond, *1933* –
Military Mayhem
1. Humour in English, 1945. Special
subjects: Military life. Anthologies.
I. Title
827'.914' 080358
ISBN 0 7104 3042 6

First published 1989
 All enquiries to:
Costello
43 High Street
Tunbridge Wells
TN1 1XL Kent

Typeset by Litho Link Limited, Welshpool, Powys, Wales
Printed and bound in Great Britain by Billings, Worcester
Jacket design by June Cummings

Contents

Mayhem in Peacetime

A World in Turmoil 1939-45

Acknowledgements

Every effort has been made to trace copyright holders. The publishers would be interested to hear from any copyright holders not here acknowledged.

George Sassoon for *The General* by Siegfried Sassoon; John Calder (Publishers) Ltd for an extract from *Blasting and Bombardiering* by P Wyndham Lewis; A P Watt Ltd for an extract from *Goodbye To All That* by Robert Graves; 'The Blocking of Zeebrugge' by Sir Archibald Hurd appeared in *Men at War* [ed] Ernest Hemingway (Branhall House/Crown Publishers NY); J M Dent & Sons Ltd for an extract from *A Touch of Genius – The Life of T E Lawrence* by M Brown and J Cave; Professor A W Lawrence for 'In The Guardroom' from *The Mint* (Jonathan Cape Ltd); Chatto & Windus for poems by Isaac Rosenberg; Rosica Colin Ltd for *At All Costs* by Richard Aldington; David Higham Associates Ltd for *Gallipoli* by Major General John Charles Frederick Fuller; the Executors of the Ernest Hemingway Estate for 'The Retreat From Caporetto' from *A Farewell To Arms* (Jonathan Cape Ltd); A P Watt Ltd on behalf of the Executors of the Estate of Robert Graves for *Armistice Day*; Macdonald & Co (Publishers) Ltd for an extract from *Wingate in Peace and War* by Major General Derek Tulloch; 'The Invaders' by Richard Hillary appeared in *Men at War* [ed] Ernest Hemingway (Branhall House/Crown Publishers Inc, NY); Unwin Hyman for two poems by Alun Lewis: 'A Troopship in the Tropics' from *Ha Ha Among the Trumpets* and 'To a Comrade in Arms' from *Raider's Dawn*; The Executors of The Michael ffolkes Estate for an extract from *ffundamental ffolkes* by Michael ffolkes (Costello); Collins Publishers for an extract from *Love and War in the Appenines* by Eric Newby; John Murray (Publishers) Ltd for 'Invasion Exercises on a Poultry Farm' by John Betjeman from his *Collected Poems*; 'Aircrew' by Brian Allwood appeared in *Resurgam 10* (The Favill Press); 'Second Autumn' by Patrick Savage appeared in *Home is the Soldier* (Fortune Press); 'After the Final Victory' by Agnes Smedley appeared in *Men at War* [ed] Ernest Hemingway (Branhall House/Crown Publishers Inc); the Peters Fraser & Dunlop Group Ltd for the 'Epilogue' from *Sword of Honour* by Evelyn Waugh (Chapman & Hall Ltd); 'Across the River and into the Ritz' by Peter Lennon appeared in *The (Manchester) Guardian* in 1964; Anthony Sheil Ltd on behalf of Professor H Tinker for an extract from *A Message From The Falklands* by Lieut David Tinker RN (Penguin); and to all other contributors to this book who gave freely of their experiences. All illustrations reproduced by kind permission of Punch Publications Ltd, except: pp 1, 3, 113, © James Morrison.

To Kay Masterson
My great, good soulmate
from West African days.

The General

Siegfried Sassoon

'Good morning; good morning!' the general said
When we met him last week on our way to the line.
Now the soldiers he smiled at are most of 'em dead,
And we're cursing his staff for incompetent swine.
'He's a cheery old card,' grunted Harry to Jack
As they slogged up to Arras with rifle and pack.

But he did for them both by his plan of attack.

Introduction

Any anthology is bound to begin as a personal affair before it becomes public. We all have favourite writers and favourite pieces of writing. Also, though, there is the question of the length of the book. Military mayhem is by no means restricted to Great Britain's armed forces; all the big warring and defending nations have had their fair share of it. One regrets, for instance, not including Napoleon's Marshal Masséna taking his mistress, Madame Leberton, on campaign dressed as a dragoon. Or on the same campaign, in Portugal, upon being woken up to rumours of Masséna's capture, Marshal Ney springing to his feet and exclaiming: 'Thank God, the Army is saved!' Or indeed, much later, the United States admiral who put his own flagship aircraft carrier on the Mississippi mudflats. However, there have to be limits; and so, with the exception of the two marvellous Hemingway pieces, this book contains poems, anecdotes and accounts about the British Military beginning with the Boer War of 1899 and ending with the Falklands conflict.

I have included a lot of the obvious big literary guns: Kipling, Wyndham Lewis, Graves, T.E. Lawrence, Hemingway, then Waugh and Betjeman. But in addition there are as quite a few solicited from previously unpublished ones, but who I felt had an appropriate contribution to make.

'Mayhem', of course, has been applied to the title of the book not in its legal sense: 'The willful and unlawful infliction of injury upon a person', but purely in its meaning that confusion can lead to chaos and sometimes amusement.

Again humour is often a very personal affair, and what amuses one will not necessarily appeal to another. Nevertheless I hope what is presented here will be suitable entertainment for both those who know the military life and others who don't. The humour itself ranges from the gently ironic to a number of absolute howlers, with many different shades in between: but none of it is fiction. And it is almost always set against the undertones and presence of actual warfare. This last fact cannot be forgotten.

In preparing the collection I owe a great debt to my own publisher's editor at Costello, Anne Cree. She has frequently fed me additions along the way, not least by some of the unpublished writers. As well as working painstakingly to give the stylistic appearance to my final selection.

So: Let us now proceed to the Mayhem....

RAYMOND HORRICKS

19th Century Mayhem

Shillin' a Day

My name is O'Kelly, I've heard the Revelly
From Birr to Bareilly, from Leeds to Lahore,
Hong-Kong to Peshawar,
Lucknow and Etawah,
And fifty-five more all endin' in 'pore'.
Black Death and his quickness, the depth and the thickness,
Of sorrow and sickness I've known on my way,
But I'm old and I'm nervis,
I'm cast from the Service,
And all I deserve is a shillin' a day.

Shillin' a day,
Bloomin' good pay –
Lucky to touch it, a shillin' a day!

Oh, it drives me half crazy to think of the days I
Went slap for the Ghazi, my sword at my side,

When we rode Hell-for-leather
Both squadrons together,
That didn't care whether we lived or we died.
But it's no use despairin', my wife must go charin'
An' me commissairin' the pay-bills to better.
So if me you be'old
In the wet and the cold,
By the Grand Metropold won't you give me a letter?

Give 'im a letter –
'Can't do no better,
Late Troop-Sergeant-Major an' – runs with a letter!
Think what 'e's been,
Think what 'e's seen,
Think of his pension an' –

GAWD SAVE THE QUEEN!

RUDYARD KIPLING

'Against Infection and the Hand of War...'

The Great Infected Blanket Scandal was widely reported in newspapers during May and June 1903. It is a typical example of the Army's disregard for hygiene and even the elementary principles of good housekeeping during the South African War, when more men died from enteric and other fevers than ever fell to Boer bullets. Florence Nightingale, then aged 83, had seven more years to live. How sad the disturbing reports filtering back from South Africa would have made her had she been able to read them. By then she was blind and living in seclusion. These reports showed how soon the army had forgotten the lessons of the Crimea, at least in the field...

The story which follows was seen in *The City Press*, the City of London's local newspaper. Naturally it emphasises the alertness of the Port Sanitary Authority – which had been the Corporation's responsibility since the Public Health Act 1872 declared them the sanitary authority for the Port of London. In 1903, incidentally, the London County Council, anxious to increase its influence, was attempting to take over this function. It all began on April 8th with a mystery outbreak of enteric (or typhoid) fever aboard the boys' reformatory ship *Cornwall,* then moored in the Thames off Purfleet and thus within the jurisdiction of the Port Sanitary Authority. By August 17th, sixteen cases had been notified and five of the boys had to be removed to the Port Isolation Hospital at Denton, below Gravesend.

The alert Dr Hancock, then acting as Port Medical Officer in the absence of his Chief, set out to find the cause. He traced it to the bedding, recently replaced by Army Surplus blankets which had been obtained from a City firm which in turn had got them from an agent in South Africa. A specimen bacteriological check on 100 blankets by Dr Klein showed that of this quantity, 98 were stained and had not been washed or disinfected before disposal by the Army – or since then, which does not say a lot for the administration of the ship. The typhoid bacillus was found in this batch.

The Port Health Authority and the City's Medical Officer of Health acted quickly. The source of supply was investigated and the names of other purchasers of blankets obtained. Dr Collingridge, the City's Medical Officer of Health (who had previously been i/c Port Health) sent letters to the MOH of each district to which the blankets had been sent, explaining the danger of widespread outbreaks of disease if the blankets were distributed. Meanwhile ships from South

Africa arriving in London's docks were checked to see if more bales of blankets were coming into the country. They were: examination showed that all were in dirty condition. Some 100,000 blankets were impounded. One consignment that slipped through was, when unpacked, found to be in such a disgusting state that the purchaser wisely had them destroyed.

The City authorities discovered that the blankets, surplus to Army requirements now that the South African War was over, had been shipped home from Cape Town. When confronted with this, the War Office said that it was contrary to regulations and promised to investigate further. Meanwhile orders were given for the destruction of the remaining stocks of condemned blankets in South Africa.

On Monday, June 7th Mr Broderick, Minister for War, made a statement which, when reading between the lines, reveals the laxity (of the men on the spot) out in Cape Town, overwhelmed by the quantity of surplus stores including 'the enormous stocks of unwashed general service blankets.' Some took fire by spontaneous combustion. The Chief Ordnance Officer then sold 80,000 of them for £1,495 (calculated at 4 1/2d per blanket). There is no indication that the purchasers did not examine the bales closely – or even use their sense of smell...

The purchasers re-sold them, which is how the reformatory ship *Cornwall* happened to acquire a consignment of these bargain blankets. Only the prompt action of the City's health department in contacting their opposite numbers in over 250 other towns prevented outbreaks of the then killer disease enteric fever from occurring throughout England.

Another newspaper report mentioned the family of a soldier who had died of the fever in South Africa. His kit was returned to them, unwashed and including the clothes he had worn in hospital. His son wore some of the clothes – and caught the disease.

Even those involved in the seizing and disinfecting of the blankets were at risk. The MOH of Stepney reported that the caretaker of the public shelter there was suffering from gastro-enteritis, contracted while assisting in the disinfecting of blankets. When one discovers that the City's MOH had taken possession of 3,095 blankets, the scale of the problem can be appreciated.

The Corporation of London Sanitary Committee did not get much change out of the War Office. They stood by the fact that the disposal of the blankets at Cape Town had been contrary to regulations. Instructions had been issued to South Africa to destroy all similar blankets in the hands of local purchasers. With regard to blankets which had already reached the United Kingdom, Mr Brodrick felt that as they had been legitimately purchased they were no longer War Department property over which he had control. Accordingly, he must leave it to the local authorities to deal with them as circumstances directed. A fine exercise in 'passing the buck': not a word about whether the culprit or culprits had been traced and punished: we are never told what happened to these gentlemen.

There is one further news item. On July 15th appeared the news that Sir Edward Ward, Permanent Under Secretary, had written to the Corporation on behalf of the War Office. He expressed his readiness to defray any of the City's expenses in tracing, disinfecting and where necessary destroying fever-infected blankets (where the infection was proven to have arisen directly from the condition of the blankets at the time of their sale by the military authorities). There is no record of the sum so paid to the Corporation, and *The City Press* commented that the Corporation should have pursued the case further by insisting that the War Office trace and punish the men responsible. After all, their incompetence and irresponsibility had involved the City in so much trouble, and put so many lives at risk.

Thereafter there is silence. Presumably nothing further was done. But I may be wrong: this story shows it from the viewpoint of one newspaper only, and a conservative one at that. The radical press of the day may well contain the sequel to this disgraceful episode – which I only hope never reached the ears of Florence Nightingale.

Postscript

There is a reference in *The City Press* of June 17, 1905 to a report published during that week on the supply of stores during the South African War.

Two years later (issue of April 13, 1907) it is evident that the Army had learned nothing from the infected blanket scandal. A report by the City's MOH referred to in this issue states that in his opinion the War Office is indifferent to the health of poor people. They have shipped back to England a large quantity of tinned goods, originally intended for the South African War. Although the goods were originally of good quality, bearing the labels of well-known manufacturers, they were by 1907 'in a rotten state.'

These goods were on sale, retail, at one halfpenny a pound. Dr Williams comments on the probable low wholesale price for which the Army authorities sold these suspect tins, if they were retailed at so low a price. He says that the attention of the Government should be further drawn to the matter and some guarantee as to the future asked for. No further reference was seen to this in the 1907 volume of *The City Press*. No reference was made to the affair of the blankets in the report.

PATRICIA O'DRISCOLL

The War To End All Wars 1914-18

from *'Blasting and Bombardiering'*

At this training camp in Dorsetshire I behaved in all respects like other Bombardiers. The evenings were passed bombardiering in the public bars, or secret upstairs parlours, of the neighbouring port. One of my bottle-companions was the Sergeant-Major. In the company of this dignitary and that of the 'quarter-bloke,' I would march down into our seaport most nights after supper to the 'house' favoured by the SM. I remember that on one occasion, this having happened as usual, we were almost trapped in a police raid.

Sitting upstairs in the seclusion of a curtained parlour, a pianola pedelling away for us, we sang drunkenly in mawkish ragtime. The 'quarter-bloke', his tunic open at the neck, his hair ruffled by the fingers of a pub *houri,* periodically turned to me, as we sat side by side on the sofa and exclaimed, 'I say, do you think we shall win!' or 'I say, what a game! Eh? What a game!' And I would turn to the Sergeant-Major and hiss, 'I say, Sergeant-Major. Do you think we shall win?' At which the Sergeant-Major would reply, 'I think so, don't you!' And I would answer, 'I feel we shall. I feel we shall!' But the SM had his rank to think about. He was not a bird to be caught in an ordinary police trap. Springing up, after cocking his ear for a moment, he was out of the door like a startled stoat. 'Jump to it! It's the MP's! Police!' he called back to us as he disappeared. Not many paces behind him I stumbled out into the pitch-black yard at the rear of the public house, and at once fell headlong over the prostrate bodies of a sailor and one of the daughters of the house. They lay parallel with the door. All the nice girls love a tar! – but I cursed and was scrambling to my feet when the quarter-bloke came cannonading over the handyman and his momentary consort, horridly indifferent to the military 'busies' blasting their way into the inner premises. Down I went a second time. When the quarter-bloke and myself emerged in the dark and empty street, the SM was half-down it, his cane glued into his armpit, his rather stiff straddle taking him off into safety with commendable celerity. When we caught him up, he looked grave. The threat to his rank had scared and sobered him. Then, hardly recovered from this, when we reached the bridge across the estuary, a searchlight burst out of the street we had just left.

The SM ordered us to take cover, and we all went over the side of the bridge as one man, and crouched out of sight till the car had passed. It was driven by a soldier and contained officers – good little SM's, as all other ranks short of the starry commissioned ones should have been in bed and asleep. Another narrow squeak for the SM crown on his sleeve. We entered the camp as usual, not by the gate where a sentry stood, but by a gap in the hedge. This was the recognised back door and invariably used by those out after hours.

After the departure for France of these earliest boon companions I continued to bellow in the field where the recruits were instructed in the elements of infantry drill. Then at last I was told that I had been recommended for a commission and left for the Field Artillery Cadet School in Exeter.

We did not correspond, the SM and myself: we were ships that passed in the night. But later on in France I met a member of my original unit. My attachment to this human group was manifested by my meticulous enquiries regarding the fate of its individual members. It was then that I heard that the Sergeant-Major had been killed within a fortnight of his arrival at the Front.

It appeared that the SM had died giving utterance to a torrent of expletives. The OC Battery was the principal target for his dying tirade; for they had been in disagreement regarding the site selected for the battery-position, which the SM regarded as too exposed. It was the usual battle between the old army, represented by the SM, and the transmogrified bank manager, the temporary officer and gentleman, who was in command of the unit. The pigheaded incompetence of this little jumped-up amateur had cost the life of a better man than himself, such was the burden of my old friend's swan-song. The ill-conceived position, chosen especially for the dug-outs, had accounted for a direct hit being registered with such promptitude upon the sumptuous rat-hole of the SM, which, in spite of all the logs and sandbags heaped on it under the direction of its occupant, could not withstand an ordinary 5.9, much less an HE or high-explosive shell.

This man was in reality a quartermaster in the old army, in appearance more like a prosperous tradesman than a warrior. He was a tall, corpulent man, with a slight stoop. On more than one occasion he remarked to me: 'I can tell you one thing, this child doesn't intend to get killed and that's that!' An ill-omened boastfulness on the part of this ill-starred SM.

•

The Romance of War:

Arrival at 'the Front' for us was not unlike arrival at a big Boxing Match, or at a Blackshirt Rally at Olympia. The same sinister expectancy, but more sinister and more electric, the same restless taciturnity of stern-faced persons assembling for a sensational and bloody event, their hearts set on a knock out. Somebody else's, of course.

•

How the Gunner Fights:

You may have asked how it is, now that I was at the Front, I was not at least firing a gun or doing something except reading *La Chartreuse de Parme* by candle-light, to earn my handsome salary. What did I do in the daytime? All that I have told you about happened at night. Was I fighting the Germans from sunrise till nightfall? Well, as a matter of fact I was doing nothing at all, most of the time.

First of all, I was a supernumerary officer, come in as a replacement for a casualty, and there was very little for me to do except hang about and smoke cigarettes.

Probably the casualty, in his turn, was a quite futile and irrational casualty – this is no reflection upon his competence, but he probably got his hit while he was performing some entirely useless routine function. He would have been better employed, it is quite likely, house-agenting or clerking somewhere in England, rather than shrouding himself in military mystery 'somewhere in France'.

The trouble about all these batteries was that they were over-burdened with officers. The Germans ran a 'five-nine' battery – our opposite number – with one officer and two or three NCO's. If the officer became a casualty, it didn't matter. While waiting for another officer, the NCO's carried on.

We had six officers in this battery. Five too many. We had no more casualties while I was there in spite of a good deal of desultory shelling. It is astonishing how many shells it takes to get one casualty.

The next battery to us, on the other hand, lost a couple of officers a week after I arrived. As usual 'reinforcements' were available almost at once, in the shape of a buxom little subaltern with cane and kitback complete, who stepped briskly out of the battery side-car, before their Mess dug-out, took a couple of steps forward, and was hit in the jaw by a splinter from a 'five-nine'. which had unexpectedly landed a few yards away. He was put back – but this time in a recumbent position – in the side-car, and returned at top-speed to the base from which he had arrived. He had spent exactly twelve minutes and a half in the Line, and would probably never see it again, as he was badly wounded.

Such are the chances of this sort of war. I was in the Line for about a year, on and off. I had shells burst within a couple of feet of my head. Splinters of every possible size have whisked around me, at every possible angle and at every variety of speed, grazing my coat, and smacking my tinhat, but I was never wounded. Yet I did not bear 'a charmed life' as our fathers called it, I was just difficult to hit, like most people. Only a few were easy – I mean with a shell.

•

It was a Day of Attack – 'somewhere in France', and the OC Battery had himself decided to go to an observation-post, and observe a bit of what was going forward. He took me with him. It was a reasonably distant one, and we saw what we had come to see without too much interference. We saw the battle: there had been no breakthrough, but a push-back. When it was evident that something had happened, and that the new front line would not be where the old front line had been, he turned to me and said, 'Well, that's that. I'm going down there, to find out where the new front line is now. Would you like to come with me?'

I expressed my desire to find myself at the side of my commanding officer.

'We shall have to fix on a new O.pip.'

That, I agreed, would undoubtably be one of the disagreeable things we should have to do.

'Yes, I think I'll go and see what's happening. Besides, I should like to have a look!'

'I should too,' I answered.

'You're sure you'd like to come? God knows what it's like. There may be no Front Line.'

'In that case we shan't be able to find it,' said I circumspectly.

'If there's one there I'll find it!' said he with great soldierly resolution, as he got up.

P. WYNDHAM LEWIS

---

from *'Goodbye to all That'*

That afternoon the company got an order from brigade to build two cruciform strong-points at such-and-such a map reference. Moodie, the company commander, and I looked at our map and laughed. Moodie sent back a message that he would be glad to obey, but would first need an artillery bombardment and considerable reinforcements, because the points selected, half-way to Martinpuich, were occupied by the enemy. Colonel Crawshay came up and verified this. He told us to build the strong-points about three hundred yards forward and two hundred yards apart. So one platoon stayed behind in the trench, and the others went out and began digging. A cruciform strong-point consisted of two trenches, each some thirty yards long, crossing at right angles in the middle; being wired all round, it looked, in diagram, like a hot-cross bun. The defenders could bring fire to bear against attacks from any direction. We were to hold these points with a Lewis gun and a platoon of men apiece.

I had the first watch that night, and periodically visited both strong-points. My way to the right-handed one took me in bright moonlight along the Bazentin-High Wood road. A dead German sergeant-major, wearing a pack and full equipment, lay supine in the middle of the sunken cart-track, his arms stretched out wide. He was a short, powerful man with a full black beard. I needed a charm to get myself past this sinister figure. The simplest way, I found, was to cross myself. Evidently a brigade of the Seventh Division had captured the road, whereupon the Germans shelled it heavily. The defenders, who were Gordon Highlanders, had begun to scrape fire-positions in the north bank, facing the Germans, a task apparently interrupted by a counter-attack. Wounded men had crawled to a number of these small hollows, thrust their heads and shoulders inside, and died there. They looked as if hiding from the black beard.

On my second visit to the strong-point, I found the trench already dug two or three feet down, and a party of Royal Engineers waiting with coils of barbed-wire for the entanglement. But work had stopped. The whisper went round: 'Get your rifles ready. Here comes Fritz!' I lay flat on my face to see better, and some seventy yards away in the moonlight, made out massed figures. I restrained the men, who were itching to fire, and sent a runner back to company headquarters asking Moodie for a Lewis gun and a flare-pistol at once. I said: 'They probably don't know we're here, and we'll get more of them if we let them come closer. They may even surrender.' The men seemed to be under no proper command: we wondered why. There had been a number of German surrenders recently at night, and this might be one on a big scale. Then Moodie arrived with the Lewis gun, the flare-pistol, and a few more men carrying rifle-grenades. Deciding to give the enemy a chance, he sent up a flare and fired the Lewis gun over their heads. The tall officer who came running towards us, his hands lifted in surrender, seemed surprised to find that we were not Germans. He claimed that he belonged to the Public Schools Battalion in our own brigade. When asked what the hell the game was, he explained that he commanded a patrol. So Moodie sent him back for a few more of his men, to make sure it was not a trick. The patrol consisted of fifty men, wandering about aimlessly between the lines, their rifles slung, and, it seemed, without the faintest idea where they were, or what information they were supposed to secure. This Public Schools Battalion was one of four or five similar ones formed in 1914. Their training had been continually interrupted by the large withdrawal of men needed to officer other regiments. The only men left, in fact, appeared to be those unfitted to hold commissions; or even to make good private soldiers. The other battalions remained in England as training corps: this alone was sent out, and proved a constant embarrassment to the brigade.

ROBERT GRAVES

The MO Visits

To add to our miseries it had poured with rain for weeks on end until our trench was knee-deep in water and the earth beneath it literally a swamp. I spent every hour dressed as usual: heavy overcoat, plus a waterproof sheet over my shoulders, plus waders, plus the inevitable equipment. What with all this and the Germans constantly reminding us of their presence, all I needed was a nasty boil on my thigh, to complete my misery, so of course I got one.

When the Medical Officer made his routine rounds I told him of my affliction, so naturally he wanted to inspect it. I had feared as much because now came the difficult part: trying to strip myself of all the equipment and clothing. It took some time, not to mention delicate manoeuvring and balancing.

But finally there I was, standing up to my knees in water, my arse bare and the doctor peering at the boil.

'Bend over', he said.

I did as instructed and that was my mistake, for I slipped and fell against the fire-step. Being saturated, it promptly gave way and deposited me in the bottom of the trench.

So there I was, deep in the water with my trousers full of mud, the boil now burst, and still as bare as a new-born babe. Then I had to journey two miles down to the First-Aid Post, complete with mud, in order to be rigged out with a dry uniform. Orders, orders....

A Rum Do

We were in the trenches at Festubert for the usual time: four days in, four days in support and eight days reserve. For the time being, Life was smiling on us. There was very little shellfire, the weather was fine and every night our rations arrived more or less on time.

And a vital part of what was brought up was our Rum ration which was carried up by the officer-in-charge and measured into each man's mess-tin. This was welcomed by all of us, but none so much as Dick Westmacott. To say that he loved it would be to put it mildly. If he could get more than his proper ration he would – and somehow he usually did. Anything you wanted done, anything at all, no matter how difficult or trivial, you only had to ask Dick and he would do it for you – in return for Rum.

None of us minded at all; it made life that little bit easier. But one evening when we had all eaten and the sun was going down, a 'stand-to' was ordered. This entailed one of us standing on the fire-step and watching for any movement on the part of the Germans. Before we knew what was happening, Dick had climbed onto the parapet.

In a moment our relief at not having to do it ourselves turned into panic as we realised that he'd gone overboard with the Rum again. He started waving his arms about, shouting that he'd kill the first Jerry bastard to dare make a move and generally creating merry hell.

How we pulled him back down into the trench in one piece I'll never know because the bullets came pouring in at him on the instant. But safe he was, though unfortunately for him his action did not go unnoticed.

When we were relieved and sent to the rear Dick was hauled up on a charge and given 7 days F.P. No.1, which meant that he was tied to a wheel for that time with his arms lashed out, as though on a crucifix. We all felt for him and knew what he was missing the most, but not one of us was able to figure out a way of getting round the rules to slip him a tot.

DON J. PRICE

from *'The Blocking of Zeebrugge'*

Following the *Thetis* came the *Intrepid,* with all her guns in full action, and Lieutenant Bonham-Carter pushed her right into the canal up to a point actually behind some of the German batteries. Here he ran her nose into the western bank, ordered his crew away, and blew her up, the engineer remaining down below in order to be able to report results. These being satisfactory, and everyone having left, Lieutenant Bonham-Carter committed himself to a Carley float – a kind of lifebuoy that, on contact with the water, automatically ignited a calcium flare. Illuminated by this, the *Intrepid's* commander found himself the target of a machine-gun on the bank, and, but for the smoke still pouring from the *Intrepid,* he would probably have been killed before the launch could rescue him.

Meanwhile the *Iphigenia,* close behind, had been equally successful under more difficult conditions. With the *Intrepid's* smoke blowing back upon her, she had found it exceedingly hard to keep her course, and had rammed a dredger with a barge moored to it, pushing the latter before her when she broke free. Lieutenant Billyard-Leake, however, was able to reach his objective – the eastern bank of the canal entrance – and here he sank her in good position, with her engines still working to keep her in place. Both vessels were thus left lying well across the canal, as aeroplane photographs afterwards confirmed; and thanks to the persistent courage of Lieutenant Percy Dean, the crews of both block-ships were safely removed.

With the accompanying motor-launch unhappily sunk as she was going in, Lieutenant Dean, under fire from all sides, often at a range of but a few feet, embarked in *Motor-Launch 282* no less than 101 officers and men. He then started for home, but, learning that there was an officer still in the water, at once returned and rescued him, three men being shot at his side as he handled his little vessel. Making a second start, just as he cleared the canal entrance, his steering-gear broke down; and he had to manoeuvre by means of his engines, hugging the side of the Mole to keep out of range of the guns. Reaching the harbour mouth he then, by a stroke of luck, found himself alongside the destroyer *Warwick,* which was thus able to take on board and complete the rescue of the block-ships' crews.

It was now nearly one o'clock on the morning of the 23rd; the main objects of the attack had been secured; and Captain Carpenter, watching the course of events, decided that it was time to recall his landing-parties. It had been arranged to do so with the *Vindictive's* siren but this, like so much of her gear, was no longer serviceable; and it was necessary to have recourse to the *Daffodil's* little hooter, so feebly opposed to the roar of the guns. Throughout the whole operation, humble as her part had been, the *Daffodil* had been performing yeoman's service, and, but for the fine seamanship of Lieutenant Harold Campbell, and the efforts of her engine-room staff, it would have been quite impossible to re-embark the marines and bluejackets from the Mole. In the normal way her boilers developed some 80lbs steam-pressure per inch; but, for the work of holding the *Vindictive* against the side of the Mole, it was necessary throughout to maintain double this pressure. All picked men, under Artificer-Engineer Sutton, the stokers held to their task in the ablest fashion; and, in ignorance of what was happening all about them, and to the muffled accompaniment of bursting shells, they worked themselves out, stripped to their vests and trousers, to the last point of exhaustion.

Nor did their colleagues on board the *Vindictive* fall in any degree short of the same high standard, as becomes clear from the account afterwards given by one of her stokers, Alfred Dingle. 'My pigeon,' he said, 'was in the boiler-room of the *Vindictive,* which left with the other craft at two o'clock on Tuesday afternoon. We were in charge of Chief Artificer-Engineer Campbell, who was formerly a merchant-service engineer and must have been specially selected for the job. He is a splendid fellow. At the start he told us what we were in for, and that before we had finished we should have to feed the fires like mad. "This ship was built at Chatham twenty years ago," he said, "and her speed is 19 knots, but if you don't get 21 knots out of her when it is wanted, well – it's up to you to do it anyway." We cheered, and he told us, when we got the order, to get at it for all we were worth, and take no notice of anybody. We were all strong fellows, the whole thirteen of us.... The *Vindictive* was got to Zeebrugge; it was just before midnight when we got alongside the Mole. We had gas-masks on then, and were stoking furiously all the time, with the artificer-engineer backing us up, and joking and keeping us in the best of spirits. Nobody could have been downhearted while he was there. There is no need to say it was awful; you know something from the accounts in the papers, although no written accounts could make you understand what it was really like... Well, there we were, bump, bump, bump against the Mole for I don't know how long, and all the time the shells shrieking and crashing, rockets going up, and a din that was too awful for words, added to which were the cries and shrieks of wounded officers and men... Several times Captain Carpenter came below and told us how things were going. That was splendid of him, I think. He was full of enthusiasm, and cheered us up wonderfully. He was the same with the seamen and men on deck... I can't help admiring the marines. They were a splendid lot of chaps, most of them seasoned men, whilst the bluejackets (who were just as good) were generally quite young men. The marines were bursting to get at the fight and were chafing under the delay all the time...While we were alongside I was stoking and took off my gas-mask, as it was so much in the way. It was a silly thing to do, but I couldn't get on with the work with it on. Suddenly I smelt gas. I don't know whether it came from an ordinary shell, but I know it was not from the smoke screen, and you ought to have seen me nip round for the helmet. I forgot where I put it for the moment, and there was I running round with my hand clapped over my mouth until I found it. In the boiler room our exciting time was after the worst was over on shore. All of a sudden the telegraph rang down, "Full speed ahead," and then there was a commotion. The artificer-engineer shouted, "Now for it; don't forget what you have to do – 21 knots, if she never does it again." In a minute or two the engines were going full pelt. Somebody came down and said we were still hitched to the Mole, but Campbell said he didn't care if we towed the Mole back with us; nothing was going to stop him. As a matter of fact, we pulled away great chunks of the masonry with the grappling irons, and brought some of it back with us. Eventually we got clear of the Mole, and there was a terrific firing up above. Mr Campbell was urging us on all the time, and we were shoving in the coal like madmen. We were all singing. One of the chaps started with, "I want to go home," and this eventually developed into a verse, and I don't think we stopped singing it for three and a half hours – pretty nearly all the time we were coming back. In other parts of the ship there wasn't much singing, for all the killed and wounded men we could get hold of had been brought on board, and were being attended to by the doctors and sick bay men. I don't know if we did the 21 knots, but we got jolly near it, and everybody worked like a Trojan, and was quite exhausted when it was all over. When we were off Dover the engineer-commander came down into the boiler-room and asked Artificer-Engineer Campbell, "What have you got to say about your men?" He replied, "I'm not going to say anything for them or anything against them; but if I was going to hell tomorrow night I would have the same men with me." '

Not until the Mole had been cleared of every man that could possibly be removed did the *Vindictive* break away, turning in a half-circle and belching flames from every pore of her broken funnels. That was perhaps her worst moment, for now she was exposed to every angry and awakened battery; her lower decks were already a shambles; and many of her navigating staff were killed or helpless. But her luck held; the enemy's shells fell short; and soon she was comparatively safe in the undispersed smoke-trails, with the glorious consciousness that she had indeed earned the Admiral's 'Well done, *Vindictive*.'

SIR ARCHIBALD HURD

The Kaiser's Realistic Dream

Being tired of his Allies he laid in his bed
And amongst other things he dreamt he was dead;
In a beautiful Coffin he was lying in state
With a guard of Germans who mourned his fate.

He wasn't long dead when he found to his cost
That his soul – like his soldiers – he also had lost;
On leaving this earth he went heavenwards straight,
And on his arrival, knocked loudly at the gate.

But the Look-out Angel in a voice loud and clear
Said 'Begone Kaiser Wilhelm! we can't have you here'
'Well,' said the Kaiser 'Since you are so uncivil,
I see no alternative but to go to the devil.'

So he turned on his heel and off he did go
At the top of his speed to the regions below;
Yet when he got there he was filled with dismay,
For whilst waiting outside he heard Old Nick say,

To his Imps, 'Now look boys to me it is clear
He's a very bad man and we don't want him here.
If once he gets in there will be no end of quarrels,
In fact I'm sure he would corrupt our good morals.'

'Oh Satan my friend,' Wilhelm loudly cried
'Excuse me for listening while waiting outside,
But if you don't admit me, where can I go?'
'Indeed' said the Devil 'I really don't know.'

'Oh do let me in, I'm feeling so cold,
If you want money, I have plenty of gold.
Let me sit in a corner no matter how hot.'
'Oh no,' said the Devil 'most certainly not,'

'We don't admit folk for their riches and self;
Here's sulphur and matches, make hell for yourself.'
With that he kicked out the Kaiser and vanished in smoke
And with this sudden shock Wilhelm awoke.

He jumped out of bed in a rage and a sweat
And said, 'Well that dream I'll never forget
That I'll not get to Heaven, I know very well,
But it's terrible to think I'm to be kicked out of hell.'

Written by a Member of the NUR
Bridgewater Branch now residing in
the 'Trenches' somewhere in France.
A.B.

from *'A Touch Of Genius: The Life of T.E. Lawrence'*

Somewhat to the surprise of his fellow undergraduates, Lawrence was conformist enough to join the University Officers' Training Corps, though, as A.P. Prys-Jones recalls, he was not its smartest member. 'He never seemed able to get his puttees wound correctly, and the hang of his uniform showed considerable eccentricity. This was suitably commented upon on one occasion by our Company Sergeant-Major, a meticulous Grenadier Guardsman. "Damned disgrace the way some of you gentlemen come on parade." ("Gentlemen" was uttered with withering sarcasm!)' Prys-Jones also noted that Lawrence was guilty of minor indiscipline at camp in preferring to take his slumber outside rather than inside the tent.

MALCOLM BROWN & JULIA CAVE

---

from *'The Mint' – In the Guard-room*

At dinner time Headquarters suddenly informed Sergeant Jenkins that he was next for guard, with every man below five feet eight in his flight. The tall men are for memorial service tomorrow. The figure gives a large surplus of shorties: however, Taffy's chosen his guard-party, and I am one.

He was angry about it. We've been so concentrated on ceremonial and cenotaph for weeks that our routine training has ceased. PT, ceremonial, school, PT, ceremonial: that's been our round, day after day. Guard-duties are a speciality and we've not even touched them. Taffy went to tell Stiffy this and said we couldn't do a guard. 'Nonsense,' replied Stiffy, 'It'll be Harry Tate of course: but I don't care for once.' 'All right,' said Taffy, 'orders is orders. Only don't call me responsible.' Behind the hut he gave us a first idea of guard-mounting; so we scrambled through the faintly silly preliminaries not too ill.

I was cast for first sentry. Along came Sergeant Major II, the decent one. On his passing I ported arms. He gave me a look, hesitated and went on. He came back through the gate. I ported again. 'Why?' he asked simply. 'Must do something, Sir, for a Sergeant Major, I suppose.' He laughed. 'Oh, you're the rag guard. Only don't do it to anyone else.'

The evening fatigue swung past, overalled, in fours. I upped my rifle to the present. Sergeant Poulton glared at me. 'What the hell do you mean, sentry, presenting to a fatigue party?' 'Token of respect, Sergeant: they do all the work.' Taffy's laugh rippled out behind me, from the shadow of the veranda. 'You **** off, Pissquick. Nobody loves you, in my squad.'

It was the night of the sergeants' mess dance. Taffy, dripping obscenities, sat on the doorstep and checked the guest-women coming in: over fifty of them. He had for each a salutation which brought giggles, a blush or a squawking laugh. In his day Taffy was a 'lad': now he prefers beer to fornication. I noticed he did not use his own manner to one single woman. Do they ever hear mens' real voices? Till two in the morning, sergeants, more or less unsteady, rolled in and out of the gates. Only eight of the fifty women had gone out of the legitimate exit by dawn. A bucket of drink was carried to the guard-room as Taffy's share of the dance's refreshment. Jock Mackay, too tight to dance, came over to help Taff drink it. The two warriors sat beside the stove, ignoring us, to chop tales of old wild service, of campaigns in India and France, of adventures in mean streets: dipping, between tales, their enamelled mugs into the beer-bucket and hiccoughing it down.

After rounds at four in the morning they sang for thirty minutes the marching songs (airs official, words the troops' own) of all the regiments they'd met. That finished, they stood up to drill. A moment before they had been swaying drunk. The touch of arms sobered them: they went through the manual from A to Z before us perfectly. More than mechanically perfect it was: a living, intelligent pattern and poem of movement. Auld Lang Syne... and Jock staggered homeward to sleep it off. Taffy fell down on our sleeping bench and was off in a moment.

Dawn came or half-came. Reveille, and the trumpeter sounded in the road by headquarters. Dimly I remembered the guard had a reveille performance. 'Sergeant,' I called, urgently shaking Taffy's shoulder. He jerked up before the call had ended, and in a moment realized the situation and our lateness. In two strides he was at the door, out of it, on the murky veranda. 'Guard attention: advance arms...' the whole procedure of morning salute he shouted into the blank mist, lest the orderly officer be on the prowl listening for us.

We guards were meanwhile struggling back from sleep off the benches, rubbing eyes and settling the night-tossed equipment into place on our shoulders. 'What's old Taffy's row all about?' wondered Park. The Sergeant stepped back to the door, mustered us with a glance of his laughter-inflamed eye and gave a last yell, 'Guard, to the guard-room, DISMISS!' 'A bloody smart lot,' he grumbled, at us crackling over his presence of mind. Out came the threatening stick and we shoved our fists into our mouths to be sober. Highly irregular, Taffy's whacking us: but we love him even for that. He's a pleasure to serve. We mollified him with the drainings of the beer-bucket. 'Good lad,' he said to me, at length.

It had fallen to little Nobby, sentry at the solitary laundry gate, to call Stiffy's batman at half-five, that the great man's cup of tea might be ready for him before work. Nobby crept timorously into the eerie black house, through the kitchen door, and incontinently lost his way. He opened one door – a box-room: another, and there was the obscure outline of a bed. He felt over it with his hands, to put them straight upon a warm face. 'Coo,' he cried, jumping back. A head, two heads, rustled up from the pillows. 'Is that Stiffy's batman?' queried Nobby, shaking: and the great known voice wrathfully clanged back 'No, it's Stiffy.'

T.E. LAWRENCE

Louse Hunting

Nudes – stark and glistening
Yelling in lurid glee. Grinning faces
And raging limbs
Whirl over the floor one fire.
For a shirt verminously busy
Yon soldier tore from his throat, with oaths
Godhead might shrink at, but not the lice.
And soon the shirt was aflare
Over the candle he'd lit while we lay.

Then we all sprang up and stript
To hunt the verminous brood.

Soon like a demons' pantomime
The place was raging.
See the silhouettes agape,

See the gibbering shadows
Mixed with the battled arms on the wall.
See gargantuan hooked fingers
Pluck in supreme flesh
To smutch supreme littleness.
See the merry limbs in hot Highland fling
Because some wizard vermin
Charmed from the quiet this revel
When our ears were half lulled
By the dark music
Blown from Sleep's trumpet.

ISAAC ROSENBERG

Marching

(As Seen from the Left File)

My eyes catch ruddy necks
Sturdily pressed back –
All red brick moving glint.
Like flaming pendulums, hands
Swing across the khaki –
Mustard coloured khaki –
To the automatic feet.

We husband the ancient glory
In these bared necks and hands.
Not broke is the forge of Mars;
But a subtler brain beats iron

To shoe the hoofs of death
(Who paws dynamic air now).
Blind fingers loose an iron cloud
To rain immortal darkness
On strong eyes.

ISAAC ROSENBERG

At All Costs

'Blast!'

Captain Hanley, commanding 'B' Company, stumbled over a broken duckboard and fell forward against the side of the trench. His tilted helmet shielded his face, but the trench wall felt oozy and soggy to his naked hand as he tried to steady himself.

'Mind that hole, Parker.'

'Very good, sir.'

He felt wet mud soaking through his breeches above the short gum boots, and his right sleeve was wet to the elbow. He fumbled in his gas bag, also wet with slimy mud, to see that the mask goggles were unbroken. OK, but he swore again with a sort of exasperated groan over the crashing bruise on his right knee.

'Are you 'it, sir?'

'No, I only fell in that mucking hole again. I've told the ser'ant-major umpteen times to get it mended. One of these days the brigadier'll fall into it and then there'll be hell to pay. Help me find my torch. I hope the bloody thing isn't broken.'

The two men groped in the darkness, fingering the slimy mud and tilted broken duckboards. Suddenly they crashed helmets.

'Sorry, sir.'

'All right, sorry.'

'Doesn't seem to be 'ere, sir.'

'Never mind, we'll look for it in the morning.'

They stumbled on cautiously. The trench was very deep (old German communication), very dark, very shell-smashed, very muddy. A black, heavy-clouded night, about an hour before dawn. Occasionally a strange ghostly glow appeared as a distant Very light was fired, and made for them a near dark horizon of tumbled shell-tormented parapet. The trench swerved, and Hanley dimly made out the shape of three crosses – Canadians. Halfway. Fifty yards further on was another turn, where a piece of corrugated iron revetment had been flung onto the top of the high parapet, where its jagged outline looked like a grotesque heraldic dragon.

It had been an ideal night for gas and would be an ideal dawn – heavy, windless, foggy – for a surprise attack. Hanley had been up and about the trenches most of the night. Since that rotten gas attack on the Somme, where he had lost twenty-three men, he took no risks. Up and down the trenches, warning the NCO's to look out for gas. Now he was on the way to his advance posts. Be there in case of an attack… Splash, squelch, splodge. Somebody coming towards them.

'Who are you?'

'Mockery.'

'Is that the word tonight, Parker?'

'Yessir.'

'That you Hanley?' Voice coming towards them.

'Hullo, Williams. I thought you were in Hurdle Alley?'

'I was, but I thought I'd have a look at these posts. They're a hell of a way from the front line.'

'I know. Damn this organization in depth. Are they all right?'

'Yes. He sent over about forty minnies, Ser'ant Cramp said, but no casualties. He was flipping over some of those flying pineapples when I left.'

From their own back areas came an irregular but ceaseless crashing of artillery. Heavy shells shrilled high above them as they swooped at enemy communications and night parties.

'Strafing the old Boche a good bit tonight,' said Williams.

'Yes, it's been quite heavy. Might almost be a windup at HQ.'

'Boche are very quiet tonight.'

'Yes; well, cheerio. Tell Thompson to keep our breakfast hot; and don't stand down until I get back.'

'Right you are, cheerio.'

Hanley visited his posts. They were established in a ruined and unrepaired German trench at the foot of a long forward slope. This had once been the British front line, but was now held only by scattered observation posts, with the main front line several hundred yards to the rear. The British bombardment increased, and the shrill scream of the passing shells was almost continuous. Very lights and rockets went up from the German lines. Hanley cursed the loss of his torch – damned difficult to get about without it. He came to the first post.

'You there, Ser'ant Tomlinson?'

A figure moved in the darkness.

'Yes, sir.'

'Anything to report?'

'No, sir.'

'Mr Williams said there were some minnies and pineapples.'

'Yes, sir, but it's very quiet sir.'

'Um. Any patrols still out?'

'No, sir, all in.'

'Very well. Carry on ser'ant.'

'Very good, sir.'

Much the same news at the other posts. Hanley returned to Number 1 post, nearest the communication trench, at dawn. The men were standing to. Hanley got on the fire-step in a shell-smashed abandoned bay, and watched with his glasses slung around his neck. The artillery had died down to a couple of batteries, when the first perceptible lightening of the air came. Hanley felt cold in his mud-soaked breeches and tunic. Very gradually, very slowly, the darkness dissipated, as if thin imperceptible veils were being rolled up in a transformation scene. The British wire became visible. In the trembling misty light No Man's Land seemed alive with strange shapes and movements. Hanley pressed cold hands on his hot eyes, puffy with lack of sleep. He looked again. Yes, yes, surely, they were climbing over the parapet and lying down in front. He seized a rifle leaning against the trench, loaded with an SOS rocket bomb. Funny Sergeant Tomlinson and the men were so silent. Perhaps he was imagining things, the same old dawn-mirage movement which had been responsible for so many false alarms. He waited a couple of minutes with closed eyes, and then looked very carefully through his glasses. Silly ass! The men coming over the parapets were the German wire pickets. He put the rifle down, glad the men had not seen him, and went round the traverse to Sergeant Tomlinson and Parker.

'Stand to for another twenty minutes, ser'ant, and then let two men from Number 2 post and two from Number 4 go and get your breakfasts.'

'Very good, sir.'

On the way back Hanley found his torch – the glass bulb was smashed; like most things in this bloody war, he reflected. Well, they'd passed another dawn without an attack – that was something. He got on a fire-step in the main line and took another look. A cloudy but rainless morning. Not a sign of life in the enemy trenches, scarcely a sound. He gave the order to stand down, and sent Parker to join his section for breakfast.

The company dugout was a large one, built as the headquarters of a German battalion. It was remarkably lousy. Hanley threw his torch, revolver-belt, and helmet on his wire and sacking bed, and sat down on a box beside a small table laid with four knives and forks on a newspaper. He felt tired, too tired even to enjoy the hot bacon and eggs which formed the infantry officers' best meal of the day. The three subalterns chatted. Hanley pushed away his plate and stood up.

'I'm going to turn in. Tell the signaller to wake me if anything important happens.'

'Right-o.'

Hanley hung up his revolver and helmet, arranged his pack as a pillow, swung himself still booted and wet onto the bed, wrapped himself in a blanket. For a few minutes he lay drowsily, listening to the throb of blood in his head and the quiet mutter of the other officers. His eyes still ached even when shut. He drowsed, then half awoke as he remembered that he had not indented for enough ammunition, decided that could wait, and – was dead asleep.

Hanley opened his eyes and lay quite still. Why were they talking so loudly? In a flash he was wide awake and swung up, sitting with his legs over the side of the bed. The colonel. Damn! Being found asleep like that! And, of course, the colonel would not know that he had been up and down the line all night. Damn! Well, never mind. He gave one dab with both hands at his rumpled hair, and stood up.

'Good morning, sir.'

'Oh, good morning, Hanley. Williams said you'd been up all night. Sorry to disturb you.'

'Quite all right, sir.'

A large-scale trench map of their sector was spread on the table, half concealing another smaller-scale artillery map of the whole district.

'Just sit down for a few minutes, Hanley. I've got important news.'

The other officers grouped beside them, gazing at the colonel and listening.

'Very important news,' the colonel went on in a slow voice, 'and not particularly pleasant, I'm afraid.'

He pulled a neat bundle of documents from his pocket, opened one labelled 'SECRET AND CONFIDENTIAL' and spread it on the table. They all gazed at it – the inexorable decree of Fate – and then again at the colonel, the agent of that Fate, of all their fates.

'That is a confidential document from Corps Headquarters. I'll tell you briefly what it is, and you can look at it afterwards. The night before last the division on our left made an identification raid, and captured a prisoner. From this and other information it seems certain that we shall be attacked – tomorrow morning – about an hour before dawn.'

Each of the four company officers drew a short imperceptible breath, glanced at each other and then quickly away. Hanley leaned his elbow on the table.

'Yes, sir?'

'It will be a surprise attack, with a very short but violent preliminary bombardment.' The colonel spoke very slowly and deliberately, looking down absently at the map, and gently twisting the lowest button of his tunic with the fingers of his right hand. 'All reports confirm our information, and the Air Force report great enemy activity behind the lines. You heard the bombardment of their communications last night.'

'Yes, sir.'

There was complete silence in the dugout, as the colonel

paused. A pile of tin plates fell with a clatter in the servants' compartment. None of the officers moved. Hanley noticed how clean the colonel's gas bag was.

'There will probably be twenty to thirty German divisions in the attack, which will be on a sixteen-mile front. We are about in the middle.'

'Yes, sir.'

The colonel moved on his box. He stretched out all the fingers of his left hand, and tapped rapidly on the table alternately with the stretched little finger and thumb.

'The Canadian Corps and several reserve divisions are being brought up at once to occupy a position about five miles to our rear. They cannot fully man the whole battle line before three tomorrow afternoon. Our duty is to delay the enemy advance until that time or longer. Our positions must be held at all costs, to the last man.'

There was a long silence. The colonel ceased drumming with his fingers and looked at them.

'Have you any questions to ask?'

'Yes, sir. Am I to leave my posts out?'

'Two hours before dawn, you will withdraw them to strengthen your own line. One section, with a sergeant and subaltern, will remain at the end of the communication trench. The subaltern will be a volunteer. His duty is to fire a green light when the German attacking line reaches him. The artillery barrage will then shorten to defend your line. You, Hanley, will have a Very-light pistol loaded with a red light, and you will fire it when the first German jumps into your trench. The object, of course, is to inform the artillery when they must shorten the defensive barrage.'

'Yes, sir.'

'Any more questions?'

'No, sir, not for the moment.'

'You'll arrange with your officers, Hanley, as to which shall volunteer to fire the green light.'

'Very good, sir.'

'And I want you to come to a conference of company officers with the brigadier at Battalion Headquarters this afternoon.'

'Very good, sir. What time?'

'Oh, make it three o'clock.'

'Very well, sir.'

The colonel rose.

'You know your battle positions, of course; but we'll discuss that this afternoon. Oh, by the bye, I'm sending up green envelopes for everyone in the company this morning. The letters must be sent down by runner at four. Of course, not a word about the attack must be mentioned either to NCO's or men until after the letters have gone.'

'Of course, sir.'

'And – er – naturally you will not mention the matter yourselves.'

'No, sir, of course not.'

'All right. Good-bye. Will you come along with me, Hanley? I should like to walk round your main defence line with you.'

'Very good, sir.'

There was silence in the dugout. They could hear the colonel and Hanley scuffing up the low dugout stairs. Williams tapped a cigarette on his case and bent down to light it at the candle burning on the table. He puffed a mouthful of smoke, with a twist to his lips.

'Well, that's that. Napoo, eh?'

'Looks like it.'

'What about a drink?'

'Right-o.'

Williams shouted:

'Thomp-sooon.'

From the distance came a muffled: 'Sir?'

A Tommy appeared in the doorway.

'Bring us a bottle of whisky and the mugs.'
'Very good, sir.'

All that day Hanley was in a state of dazed hebetude, from which he emerged from time to time. He felt vaguely surprised that everything was so much as usual. There were sentries at their posts, runners going along the trenches, an occasional airplane overhead, a little artillery – just the ordinary routine of trench warfare. And yet within twenty-four hours their trenches would be obliterated, he and thousands with him would be dead, obliterated, unless by some chance, some odd freak, he was made a prisoner. He heard repeated over and over again in his head the words: 'Position must be held at all costs, position must be held at all costs.' He felt suddenly angry. Held at all costs! All jolly fine and large to write from the safety of Montreuil, but what about those who had to make good such dramatic sentiments with their lives? The front was ridiculously denuded of men – why, his own under-strength company held very nearly a battalion front, and had a flank to guard as well. If they fought like madmen and stood to the last man, they might hold up three waves – an hour at most. And they were asked to hold out for nearly twelve hours! Ridiculous, good God, ridiculous! He found the colonel shaking him by the arm.

'What's the matter with you, Hanley? You don't seem to hear what I'm saying.'

'I beg your pardon, sir I—'

'I think you ought to bring a Lewis gun up to this point. You've got an excellent field of fire here.'

'Very good, sir.'

Hanley noted the change to be made in his field service message book. They walked on, and the colonel made various other suggestions – so many orders – which Hanley duly noted. The colonel paused at the corner of the communication trench leading to Battalion Headquarters. He waved to the orderlies to stand apart.

'We'll discuss the general plan of defence at the conference this afternoon. Make a note of anything that occurs to you, any information you want, and bring it up.'

'Right, sir.'

The colonel hesitated a moment.

'It's a very difficult position, Hanley, I know, but we must all do our duty.'

'Of course, sir.'

'I shall lead the counter-attack of the Reserve Company myself.'

'Yes, sir.'

'A great deal depends on our putting up a good show.'

'Yes, sir.'

'I suggest you go round to the dugout and speak to all your men this evening. Put a good face on it, you know. Tell them we are all prepared, and shall easily beat off the attack, and that reinforcements are being hurried up to relieve us. And above all impress upon them that these trenches must be held at all costs.'

'Very good, sir.'

The colonel held out his hand.

'I may not get another opportunity to speak to you in private. Good-bye, and the best of luck. I know you'll do your duty.'

'Thank you, sir. Good-bye.'

'Good-bye.'

When Hanley stooped under the low entrance of the dugout chamber, the three subalterns were seated round the table with flushed cheeks, talking loudly. The whisky bottle was more than half-empty. A sudden spurt of anger shot through him. He strode up to the table and knocked the cork level with the top of the bottle neck with one hard smack of his hand. He spoke harshly:

'What's this nonsense?'

Williams, the eldest of the three subalterns, answered, half-defiantly, half-ashamedly:

'We're only having a drink. Where's the harm?'

'Only a drink! Before lunch! Now, look here, you fellows. The whisky that's left in that bottle is all that's going to be drunk in this mess between now and dawn tomorrow. Understand? One of the damned stupidities of this damned war is that every officer thinks it's the thing to be a boozer. It isn't. The men don't drink. They get a tablespoon of rum a day. Why should we make sots of ourselves? We're responsible for their lives. See? And we're responsible for these trenches. We've got to leave 'em on stretchers or stay here and manure 'em. See? We've got a bloody rotten job ahead of us, a stinking rotten job, and I wish those who ordered it were here to carry out their own damned orders. But they're not. Not bloody likely. But the people at home trust us. We're responsible to them, first and foremost. We took on the job, and we've got to carry it out. And carry it out dead bloody sober. Got me?'

The men were silent, looking sheepishly at the newspaper on the table with its wet rings from mug bottoms. Hanley took an empty mug and tossed some of the whisky from Williams' mug into it.

'Drink up. Here's hell!'

They drank.

Hanley shouted:

'Thomp-soooon!'

Thompson appeared in the door.

'Take those mugs away.'

'Very good, sir.'

'How many bottles of whisky have you?'

'Three, sir.'

'Bring them here, and a sandbag.'

'Very good, sir.'

Hanley scribbled a few words in his message book, and tore out the slip. He put the bottles in the sandbag.

'Parker!'

Parker in his turn appeared.

'Sir?'

'Take that sandbag down to Battalion HQ. Give it to one of the officers, and bring back his signed receipt.'

'Very good, sir.'

The other officers exchanged glances. Williams who had his back turned to Hanley, made a grimace of derision. The others frowned at him.

Hanley was busy throughout the day, making arrangements, giving orders, attending the conference – which lasted a long time – and going round to speak to the men. He only had time to write a very brief letter to his wife, enclosing one still briefer for his father. He wrote calmly, almost coldly in his effort to avoid emotion and self-pity. He even managed to squeeze out a joke for each letter. As soon as they were finished the two letters vanished in the open sandbag containing the company mail, and the runner started at once for Headquarters. Somehow it was a relief to have those letters gone. The last links with England, with life, were broken. Finished, done with, almost forgotten. It was easier to carry on now.

But was it? There was that damned business of the volunteer subaltern. Hanley rubbed his clenched fist against his cheek, and found that he had forgotten to shave. He called his servant and told him to bring some hot water in a cigarette tin. Shaving for the last time. Hardly worth it, really. Still, must be done. Morale, and all that.

He shaved carefully. One of the subalterns went out to relieve the officer on duty. One was asleep. Williams was writing a situation report. Hanley bit the back of his hand hard, then shoved both hands in his breeches pockets, looking at Williams' bent head.

'Williams!'

Williams looked up.

'Yes?'

'There's this business of the volunteer to –'

'Oh, that's all settled.'

'Settled!'

'Yes. I'm going.'

'You're going! But you've only been married two months.'

'Yes. That's why I thought I'd like to get it over with as quickly as possible.'

'But I was going to put your platoon at the end of Hurdle Alley. You might just be able to get back to battalion, you know.'

'And feel a swine for the rest of my life – which would be about two hours? Thanks. No, I'd rather get it over, if you don't mind, Hanley.'

'Oh, all right.'

They were silent. The Hanley said:

'Well, I'll just go and talk to the men... er... So long.'

'So long.'

All working parties were cancelled to give the men as much rest as possible, but there was inevitably a lot of extra work, bringing up ammunition, rations and water. As soon as dusk fell the whole Reserve Company and some pioneers came up to strengthen the wire. The British artillery was ceaselessly active. Hardly a shot came from the German lines – an ominous sign.

After dinner Hanley lay down to sleep for a few hours. Must be as fresh as possible. He wrapped the blanket up to his chin and shut his eyes. The other three off duty were lying down, too. But Hanley could not sleep. It was all so strange, so strange and yet so ordinary. Just like any other night, and yet the last night. Inevitably the last night? How could they escape, with orders to hold on at all costs? Half of them would go in the bombardment, which would be terrific. Bombs, bullets and bayonets would finish off the rest. The dugouts would be wrecked with bombs and high explosive charges. A few of the wounded might be picked up later. A few of the men might escape down Hurdle Alley after the officers were gone. But no, the NCO's could be relied on to hold out to the last. They were done for, napoo. No *aprés la guerre* for them – bon soir, toodle-oo, good-byeeee. The silly words repeated and repeated in his brain until he hated them. He opened his eyes and gazed at the familiar dugout. His wire bed was at an angle to the others, and he could see the shapes of Williams and the two other officers muffled up silent in their blankets – as still and silent as they would be in twenty-four hours' time. There was the candle burning in the holder roughly bent from a tin biscuit box. The flame was absolutely steady in the airless, earthy smelling dugout. There were the boxes for seats, the table with its maps, tins of cigarettes, chits, and the five mugs beside the whisky bottle for the last parting drink. The bare, murky walls of chalk were damp and clammy-looking with condensed breath. The revolvers, helmets, and gas bags were hung at the bed-heads. He listened to the other men breathing, and felt an absurd regret at leaving the dugout to be smashed. After all, that and other dugouts like it were the only home they had known for months and months. Breaking up the happy home! He became aware that he felt a bit sickish, that he had been feeling like that for several hours, and pretending not to.

He gently drew his wrist from under the blanket and looked at his luminous watch. Eleven thirty-five. He had to be up at two – must get some sleep. With almost a start he noticed that Williams was looking at his own watch in the same stealthy way. So he couldn't sleep either. Poor devil. Profoundly, almost insanely in love with that wife of his. Poor devil. But still, for the matter of that, so was Hanley in love with his wife. His heart seemed to turn in his body, and he felt an acute pain in the muscles above it as he suddenly realized fully that it was all over, that he would never see her again, never feel her mouth pressed to his, never again touch her lovely, friendly body. He clutched his hand over his face until it hurt to prevent himself from groaning. God, what bloody agony! O God, he'd be a mass of dead rotting decay, and she'd still be young and beautiful and alert and desirable, O God, and her life would run on, run on, there'd be all the grief and the sorrowing for her and tears in a cold widowed bed, O God, but the years would run on and she'd still be young and desirable, and somebody else would want her, some youngster, some wangler, and youth and her flesh and life would be clamorous, and her bed would no longer be cold and widowed. O God, God. Something wet ran down his cheek. Not a tear, but the cold clammy sweat from his forehead. God, what agony!

Hanley suddenly sat up. If he was suffering like that, Williams must be suffering, too. Better to get up and pretend to talk than lie and agonize like that. He got out of bed. Williams raised his head:

'What's up. It isn't two, is it?'

The other men looked up, too, showing that neither of them had been asleep. Hanley shivered and rubbed his hands to warm them in the chill dugout.

'No, only five to twelve. But I couldn't sleep. Hope I don't disturb you. Benson must be relieved in a few minutes,' he added, inconsequently.

The other three rolled out of bed and stood stretching and rubbing their hands.

'Too cold to sleep in this damned damp place,' said one of them.

'What about a drink?'

'If you have it now, you can't have it later on,' said Hanley. 'Better wait until two.'

Williams put on his equipment and helmet and went up to relieve Benson. The others sat on the boxes trying to talk. Benson came down.

'Anything on?' asked Hanley casually.

'Lots of lights, ordinary strafing on their side. A hell of a bombardment from our side.'

'Perhaps if they see we've got wind of it, they'll postpone the attack?' suggested the youngest officer.

'Rot,' said Benson. 'They know jolly well that all this part of the line has been denuded to feed the Fifth Army. They'll attack, all right.'

They were silent. Hanley looked at his watch. Five past twelve. How damnably slow the time went; and yet these were their last minutes on earth. He felt something had to be done.

'Let's have a hand of bridge.'

'What, tonight, now?'

'Well, why not? It's no good sitting here grumping like owls, and you don't suggest a prayer meeting, do you?'

The last last suggestion was met with oaths of a forcible nature. Hanley cleared the table and threw down the cards.

'Cut for deal.'

Just before two, Hanley slipped into his breeches pocket the ten francs he had won, and stood up. He put on trench coat and muffler, tried his broken torch for about the twentieth time, then threw it down disgustedly and fitted on his equipment. The subaltern who was to relieve Williams on trench duty was already dressed and waiting. Hanley put on his hat and turned to the others.

'I'll come round and see you after you've taken up battle

positions; but if by any chance I don't see you again – cheerio.'

'Cheerio.'

They found Williams, his runner, and a sergeant waiting in the trench outside the dugout entrance.

'Anything doing?'

'Nothing particular. I went on patrol. Their wire's got gaps cut, with knife-rests in the gaps, all the way along.'

'Um.'

'Lots of signal rockets, too.'

'I see. Our artillery seems to have ceased altogether.'

'Saving ammunition for the show.'

'Be more sensible to strafe now while the Boche is taking up battle positions.'

'Oh, well, that's the staff's job, not ours.'

Hanley, Williams, the sergeant, two runners, started for the Outpost Line. The trench was drier, the night not so dark, with faint stars mistily gleaming among light clouds. Weather clearing up – just the Boche's luck again. The five men moved along without talking, absorbed partly in a strange anxious preoccupation, partly in keeping upright on the slippery trench. Hanley and Williams, of course, knew the full extent of their danger, had faced the ultimate despair, passed beyond revolt or hope. The sergeant still hoped – that he might be wounded and taken prisoner. The two men only knew they were 'in for a show'. All were dry-mouthed, a little sickish with apprehension, a litle awkward in all their movements; the thought of deserting their posts never even occurred to them.

They passed the three Canadian crosses, distinctly outlined on the quiet sky; then the dragon piece of corrugated iron. At the end of the communication trench they found waiting the men from the four posts, under a sergeant. Hanley spoke in low tones – there might be advance patrols lying just outside their wire.

'All your men present, ser'ant?'

'Yes, sir.'

'Right. You know your orders. See that each section joins its own platoon, and then report to your own platoon commander. Don't waste time.'

'Very good, sir.'

The line of men filed past them in the darkness. For the hundredth time Hanley noticed the curious pathos of fatigue in these silent moving figures – the young bodies somehow tired to age and apathy. When they had gone he took Williams a little aside.

'If I were you, I should see that each of you occupies a separate bay. Get in the first bay yourself, then the runner, then the sergeant. They won't dare try to bolt back past you. Besides – er – there's more chance if you're spread out.'

'I was wondering what happens if all three of us are knocked out before the Boche actually gets into the trench, and so no green light is fired?'

'Oh, we must risk that. Besides, there are similar volunteer parties on every company front.'

'I see.'

'I took a compass bearing from the fire-step outside Company HQ yesterday, so I shan't miss your light. I expect they'll be on us ten minutes later. Perhaps we'll beat off the first two or three attacks.'

'Yes. Perhaps.'

They were silent. Then Hanley made an effort.

'Well, good-bye, old man. Best of luck.'

'Best of luck, good-bye.'

They were too shy and English even to shake hands.

It was past three when Hanley and Parker got back to their own line and found the whole company standing to in battle positions. Hanley kept his signallers on the first floor of the big dugout. He sent off to Battalion Headquarters the code message which meant they were in battle positions and all ready. He took a candle and went down to the lower dugout, where they had spent so many nights. It looked barer and damper than ever, empty except for the bare sacking beds, the boxes, the table.

Outside in the trench the air was moist and fresh. He took two Very pistols, one loaded with green, one with red, and laid them on either side of him on the parapet. Hanley was at the extreme left of the bay, with two riflemen to his right. Twenty yards to his left was the communication trench leading to the outpost line, now blocked with wire and knife-rests, and guarded by a bombing section.

A signaller came up from the dugout with a message. Hanley went down and read it by the light of a candle. He noticed the bowed back and absorbed look of a signaller tapping out a message on a Fullerphone. The message he had received simply reiterated the order that their positions were to be held at all costs. Hanley felt angry, screwed up the piece of paper and stuffed it into his pocket. Damn them, how many more times did they think that order had to be given? He returned to the trench, and resumed his watch.

3.50 A.M. One battery of German guns languidly firing on back areas – pretence that all was as usual.

3.52 A.M. Signal rockets all along the German line. Then silence.

3.55 A.M. Two miles to his right a fierce bombardment, stretching over several miles. The battle had begun.

3.57 A.M. Two miles to his left another bombardment. The British artillery on their own front opened up a defensive barrage.

4 A.M. With a terrific crash, which immediately blotted out the roar of the other bombardments, the German artillery

on their own front came into action. Hanley half-recoiled. He had been in several big bombardments, and thought he had experienced the utmost limit of artillery. But this was more tremendous, more hellish, more appalling than anything he had experienced. The trench of the outpost line was one continuous line of red, crashing trench mortars and shells. The communication trench was plastered with five-nines. Shells were falling all along their own line – he heard the sharp cry 'Stretcher-bearer' very faintly from somewhere close at hand.

The confusion and horror of a great battle descended on him. The crash of shells, the roar of guns, the brilliant flashes, the eerie piercing scream of a wounded man, the rattle of the machine guns, the Lewis guns, the two riflemen beside him madly working the bolts of their rifles and fumbling as with trembling hands they thrust in a fresh clip of cartridges – all somehow perceived, but thrust aside in his intense watch. A green light went up about half a mile to the left, then another a little nearer. Hanley stared more intently in the direction of Williams's post – and found himself saying over and over again without knowing he was saying it: 'O God, help him, O God, help him, O God, help him.'

Suddenly two green lights appeared, one fired straight up as a signal – probably Williams – the other almost along the ground, as if fired at somebody – probably the runner, wounded or in panic. Sergeant dead, no doubt – Williams and his runner dead, too, by now. Hanley fired a green light. Two minutes later the British barrage shortened.

Hanley grasped the Very pistol loaded with red. Their turn now.

'Stretcher-bearer, stretcher-bearer.'

Crash! A shell right on their bay.

Hanley staggered and felt a fearful pain in his right knee where a shell splinter had hit him. In the faint light of dawn he saw vaguely that one of the riflemen lay huddled on the fire-step, leaving his rifle still on the parapet; the other man had been blown backwards into the trench, and lay with his feet grimly and ludicrously caught in a torn piece of revetment. His helmet had been knocked from his head.

Faint pops of bombs to his immediate left – they were coming up the communication trench. He peered into the steel-smashed light of dawn, but saw only smoke and the fierce red flash of explosions.

Suddenly, to his left, he saw German helmets coming up the communication trench – they had passed the wire barrier! He looked to his right – a little knot of Germans had got through the wire – a Lewis gun swept them away like flies. He felt the blood running down his leg.

Somebody was standing beside him. A voice, far off, was speaking:

'Bombing attack beaten off, sir.'

'Very good, carry on.'

'There's only two of us left, sir.'

'Carry on.'

'Very good, sir.'

More Germans on the right; another, longer row coming up the communication trench. Then, suddenly, Germans seemed to spring up in every direction. Hanley fired six shots from his Webley at those in front. He saw others falling hit, or jumping into the trench on either side.

A red light shot straight up in the air. A second later two bombs fell in the bay. A torn, crumpled figure collapsed sideways. The Germans reorganized, while the moppers-up did their job.

RICHARD ALDINGTON

Everything is very simple in War, but the simplest thing is difficult. These difficulties accumulate and produce a friction which no man can imagine exactly who has not seen war.

Gallipoli

The stalemate which followed the battle of the Marne was almost as decisive in its results as was the battle itself. First, Germany turned Eastwards, and from then onwards until February, 1916, she launched her legions against Russia, which country began to collapse before 1914 had run its course. Then, as I shall soon show, Great Britain also turned East, not because her small army possessed a superabundance of power, but because the German fleet refused to sacrifice itself on the British naval altar. In the middle of October the first Battle of Ypres opened and was continued until November 21st, during the whole of which time Sir John French's Expeditionary Force had to hold on to its parapets by its fingertips.

Worse still, in London there was no thinking military head. The War Office had been denuded of trained Staff officers, and, according to Mr Lloyd George, British statesmen were second-rate. Not until November did Mr Asquith, the Prime Minister, decide to establish a War Council, whilst the Committee of Imperial Defence remained inoperative. Mr Churchill, then First Lord of the Admiralty, exclaimed: 'Confronted with this deadlock, military art remained dumb; the Commanders and their General Staffs had no plan except the frontal attack which all their experience and training had led them to reject; they had no policy except the policy of exhaustion.' And Mr Lloyd George writes on December 31: 'I can see no signs anywhere that our military leaders and guides are considering any plans for extricating us from our present unsatisfactory position.'

Is this fair criticism? I do not think so, because the truth is that Great Britain was in no way prepared for a war on one front, let alone two or three. It may well be correct, as Lloyd George says, that the soldier did not understand his art, yet should not the chief blame be loaded upon the shoulders of the Parliamentary system which could neither prepare for a war nor direct its course?

The fact is, a fact which must not be overlooked, that, as in 1775, so far as England was concerned this was a Parliamentary war – a war of amateur strategists. Mr John North, in an illuminating book on the Gallipoli campaign, says: 'I have never been able to understand the professionals' sneer at the amateur strategist.' No wonder, for he adds: 'War is a matter of common sense,' which is exactly what amateurs lack. They can readily conceive a campaign, but overlook that between conception and execution yawns an illimitable gulf of detail and technique. For example: in some long-forgotten year of the primeval world Daedalus conceived the idea of human flight; yet it was not until 1903 that two practical mechanics, Wilbur and Orville Wright, solved that problem by producing the first heavier-than-air machine. The truth is that there were far too many amateur strategists. Admiral Wemyss writes: 'everything is done at home in watertight compartments; no Minister has the slightest idea of what his neighbours and colleagues are doing... the men at the head of affairs are ignorant of all technique; they think they only have to say "Do it" and it is done – wrong.' And, a little later on, what does General Sir William Robertson say? 'The Secretary of State for War was aiming at decisive results on the Western Front; the First Lord of the Admiralty was advocating a military expedition to the Dardanelles; the Secretary of State for India was devoting his attention to a campaign in Mesopotamia... the Secretary for the Colonies was occupying himself with "several small wars" in Africa; and the Chancellor of the Exchequer, Mr Lloyd George, was attempting to secure the removal of a large part of the British Army from France to some Eastern Mediterranean theatre.' Five active tentacles and no head – such was the British strategical polyp.

Strange as it may seem, the conception of the Gallipoli or Dardanelles campaign pre-dated the Battle of the Marne. On August 20th, M. Venizelos, the Greek Prime Minister, with the full approval of King Constantine, placed all the military and naval resources of Greece at the disposal of the Entente Powers; nevertheless, for fear of antagonising Turkey, Sir Edward Grey, British Foreign Secretary, rejected this offer. Notwithstanding this, on the 31st Mr Churchill discussed the problem with Lord Kitchener, Secretary of State for War, and the following day 'Mr Churchill asked the Chief of the Imperial General Staff to appoint two officers to examine and work out, with two officers from the Admiralty, "a plan for the seizure of the Gallipoli peninsula, by means of a Greek army of adequate strength, with a view to admitting a British fleet to the Sea of Marmora."' Thus the tension between cross-purposes started, to be complicated by the fact that, at this time, Lord Fisher, First Sea Lord, was pushing for a landing in the Baltic. Such an operation required troops, and Kitchener had none to spare, consequently the Dardanelles project gained in favour, yet was complicated by the fact that the Greeks now refused to budge unless Bulgaria agreed to declare war on Turkey. So the idea was shelved, until towards the end of November two Australian Divisions arrived in Egypt; whereupon Mr Churchill once again revived it, ordering the transports which had carried them to remain in Egypt 'in case they are required for an expedition.' Meanwhile, on his authority, a senseless operation of war was carried out: On November 3rd, two days after the British Ambassador left Constantinople, the Admiralty ordered the bombardment of the Dardanelles forts. This bombardment, said Jevad Pasha (Commandant of the fortresses) after the war, 'warned me and I realised that I must spend the rest of my time in developing and strengthening the defences by every means.'

From now onwards Mr Churchill became fanatically obsessed with the idea of occupying Constantinople, in which city was located the sole munition factory in Turkey. There can be little doubt that so far as pure strategy is concerned he was right. Later, on June 5th, 1915, he said: 'Through the Narrows of the Dardanelles and across the ridges of the Gallipoli peninsula lie some of the shortest paths to triumphant peace.' Yet this strategy was amateurish, because 'he saw the huge prize, and tried to seize it with inadequate means.' The execution of his idea depended upon Greek support, which was not forthcoming; further, England was not capable of fighting on two fronts, for though it was comparatively easy for the War Office to raise men, it was impossible in a few weeks or months to create an efficient corps of officers. Further still, the British Army was not equipped or trained for a campaign in a theatre such as Gallipoli.

The truth is that the brilliance of his conception blinded him to the requirements of its execution. Mr North says: 'The responsibility for the inauguration of the Dardanelles campaign rests upon Mr Winston Churchill' – which is true. And Admiral Keyes says: 'But if he had not committed the Government to the enterprise, they would never have looked at it' – which is also true. In brief, and against the opinion of Sir William Robertson, who became Chief of the Imperial General Staff in December, he forced his Dardanelles card on the Government, the Government being incapable of playing the game. The result was that the British Empire not so much drifted, but was pushed into a campaign which in the end proved as disastrous as that of Saratoga.

On January 1st, 1915, two papers were submitted to the War Council; the first by Lieutenant-Colonel Maurice

Hankey, Secretary of the Council, and the second by Mr Lloyd George. In the former it was suggested that Germany could be struck more easily through Turkey, and that should the Black Sea be re-opened, the price of wheat would fall and 350,000 tons of shipping would be released. The latter considered that the Eastern operation should be directed against Austria and be based on Salonika; but this suggestion was set aside, because it demanded a considerable number of troops.

Next day 'a telegram of momentous consequence' was received from the British Ambassador at Petrograd, notifying the Cabinet of the critical position of the Russian forces in the Caucasus, when, in fact, the crisis there was all but over; whereupon Kitchener telegraphed in reply: 'Please assure the Grand Duke that steps will be taken to make a demonstration against the Turks,' whilst Fisher set before Mr Churchill a grandiose plan. He strongly supported an attack on Turkey if it could be carried out immediately: 75,000 men from France were to land at Besika Bay; another landing was to be made at Alexandretta and a demonstration at Haifa. 'Simultaneously the Greeks should be landed on the Gallipoli peninsula, the Bulgarians should be induced to march on Adrianople, and the Rumanians to join the Russians and Serbs in an attack on Austria. Finally, Admiral Sturdee should at the same time force the Dardanelles with ships of the Majestic and Canopus class.'

Blowing the froth off this tankard of strategic ale, Churchill gulped down the idea of forcing the Dardanelles with old battleships, and telegraphed to Vice-Admiral Carden, commanding at the Dardanelles: 'Do you consider the forcing of the Dardanelles by ships alone a practicable operation?' To which, on the 5th, Carden answered: 'I do not consider Dardanelles can be rushed. They might be forced by extended operations with a large number of ships.'

This was good enough for Mr. Churchill, and though

Lord Fisher, Admiral Sir Henry Jackson and Mr Lloyd George were vehemently opposed to this proposal, in it Churchill saw the means of winning over Lord Kitchener, because it would not entail the use of troops. 'So Lord Kitchener swung round to the Dardanelles plan,' writes Mr. Lloyd George, 'and that settled it.'

On the 13th, Churchill brought his project before the War Council, pointing out that if progress were not made, 'the bombardment could be broken off and the fleet could steam away,' which consideration won over the Government. Then, on the 15th, he telegraphed to Admiral Carden: 'The sooner we can begin the better... Continue to perfect your plan': and four days later he cabled the Grand Duke Nicholas, informing him that the Government had determined to force the Dardanelles. At length, on the 28th, when the War Council met again, though Lord Fisher opposed the project and urged the greater value of his Baltic scheme, Lord Kitchener considered the naval attack of vital importance; Mr Balfour could not imagine a more helpful operation, and Sir Edward Grey thought it would settle the attitude of the whole of the Balkans. Not a soldier was to be used, the navy alone was to force the Dardanelles and seize Constantinople.

Thus the proposal passed into the realm of action, and apparently became public property, for Lord Bertie, then British Ambassador in Paris, writes: 'The Dardanelles Expedition was known only to the inner ring: Louis Mallett heard of it at a dinner from Leo (Leopold) de Rothschild, who had learnt it from Alfred de R. (Rothschild) who may have picked up the information in the course of his daily visit to Kitchener, at the War Office and 10 Downing Street. There is no such thing as a secret nowadays.'

No sooner had the naval attack been agreed upon than the Salonika project was revived, and though it was turned down, out of it emerged the old question whether the ships should not be supported by a military force. So, on February

16th, the War Council met again to review this question, and a decision was made to send out the 29th Division as well as to despatch troops from Egypt. Thus were the foundations of the military attack laid. Then, three days later, Kitchener said he could not spare the 19th Division, so in its stead were substituted the Australian and New Zealand divisions in Egypt. Mr. Churchill, now considering that at least 30,000 men would be required, insisted for the first time that it 'would be impossible for the fleet to keep the Dardanelles open for merchant shipping.' Next, on the 24th, Mr Lloyd George asked him whether, should the naval attack fail, the army would carry out a land attack, and his answer was 'No!'

The muddle in execution was now complete, and on it the first gigantic blunder was founded – namely, the futile naval bombardments of the outer forts on February 19th and 25th. Though this operation was inconclusive, sufficient damage was done to allow of small parties 'of 50 to 100 sailors and marines' landing on the 26th, and leisurely blowing to pieces 'all the guns in Sedd-el-Bahr, as well as in the two forts on the Asiatic side,' at the cost of one killed and six wounded. Thus it came about that no sooner had the War Council made up their mind not to use troops than they decided to use them, and then, having arrived at this decision, they decided to carry out the naval attack without them. Instead of waiting until the army was ready to follow up the naval barrage, on the day following the bombardment Lord Kitchener warned General Maxwell, GOC Egypt, to hold in readiness 30,000 Australian and New Zealand troops under Lieutenant-General Sir W R Birdwood 'to embark about the 9th March, in transports sent from England, "to assist the navy... and to occupy any captured forts."' Then, suddenly, on the 24th, the War Council realised that, on account of Mr. Churchill's impetuosity, they had precipitated the operation into a bottomless bog, or as the official historian writes: 'If a success at the Dardanelles could win the Balkans to the Entente, a failure would have the opposite effect. The opening of the bombardment had attracted such world-wide attention that, for the sake of British prestige, the enterprise must be carried through, no matter what the cost... Mr Churchill argued that the country was absolutely committed to seeing the Dardanelles attack through.'

On March 4th further landings were attempted which were met by strong opposition, and all efforts to sweep the minefields were met by heavy fire directed by searchlights. The Turks were now wide awake, so on the 5th the *Queen Elizabeth* and other warships opened an indirect bombardment on the forts in the Narrows, and continued to do so until the 12th, each shell fired bringing home to Turkey the impending danger.

Whilst this bombardment was in progress, the next gigantic blunder was made, this time by Russia, for whose benefit the operation had so largely been undertaken. On the 1st M. Venizelos informed the British Government that he was ready to land three divisions on the Gallipoli peninsula; in the circumstances this offer was as miraculous as Abraham's ram. Forthwith it was communicated to Russia, who, on the 3rd, replied: 'The Russian Government could not consent to Greece participating in operations in the Dardanelles, as it would be sure to lead to complications...' These centred on who should possess Constantinople, which city the British Government had promised to Russia as her share of the world-booty once the war was won. On the 7th the Venizelos Government fell, and, on the 12th, the day the bombardment ceased, this piece of political backshish was made public. Thus Russia seized the shadow and Great Britain swallowed the substance.

On the day this suicidal refusal was made the War Council met again, and once more Kitchener refused to release the 29th Division. Then, on the 5th, he received a telegram from General Birdwood saying, 'I am very doubtful if the Navy can force the passage unassisted,' whereupon he changed his mind, and, assuming full responsibility for the military attack, he took over the Royal Naval Division, and, on the 16th, the 29th Division sailed.

This decision, three weeks too late, was followed by the third gigantic blunder. Having made up his mind to send the 29th Division out, a veritable scramble followed. Looking around for a General-in-Chief, he selected Sir Ian Hamilton, an officer of much war experience, who had taken part in seven colonial wars in Afghanistan, S. Africa, Egypt, Burma and India, and who in 1904–5 had accompanied the Japanese in the field. On discussing the situation with him, Lord Kitchener said: 'If the fleet gets through, Constantinople will fall of itself and you will have won not a battle but the war'; yet he gave him no instructions, instead an out-of-date map, and hurried him off on the 13th, as if he were in command of a corporal's patrol. Arriving at Mudros on the 17th, General Hamilton found that Admiral J.M. de Robeck had that day replaced Admiral Carden, and that, when the 29th Division had left England, the embarkation authorities, imagining that it would land at a friendly harbour, had loaded the ships in such a way that the troops could not disembark in fighting order; therefore the transports would have to be completely discharged and reloaded. As this could not be carried out at Mudros, it had to be done at Alexandria, which meant another three weeks' delay.

The day Lord Kitchener selected Sir Ian Hamilton to command the expedition, Mr Churchill, instead of waiting for a combined operation to be elaborated, telegraphed Admiral Carden: 'We suggest for your consideration that a point has now been reached when it is necessary... to overwhelm the forts at the Narrows at decisive range by the fire of the largest number of guns...' Such was the fourth gigantic blunder. The attack was made on the 18th, when three battleships were lost through running into an unswept minefield; whereupon de Robeck informed the Admiralty that he intended to postpone his next effort until about the middle of April, when the army would be ready to act. The truth would appear to be, as Admiral Keyes writes: 'He never really wished to risk his ships again in another naval attack, after the losses of the 18th March, and he welcomed the opportunity of combining with the army in an operation which promised success without hazard to the fleet.' Thus it came about that the army was called upon to pull Mr Churchill's naval chestnuts out of the fire.

Whilst the Turks were digging for their lives, the 29th Division disembarked at Alexandria, where it was found that it had been equipped for mobile warfare in a well-roaded country, yet was deficient of guns, gun and rifle ammunition, hospital requirements and trench stores. As to secrecy there was none, one of Sir Ian Hamilton's Staff receiving 'an official letter from London, sent through the ordinary post, and addressed to the "Constantinople Field Force." '

On the 22nd a conference was held on the *Queen Elizabeth;* of it General Hamilton writes: 'The moment we sat down de Robeck told us he was quite clear he could not get through without the help of all my troops... the fat (that is us) is fairly in the fire.' The idea of landing at Bulair was set aside, not only because it was known to be entrenched, but because 'the main communications of the Turkish divisions in the peninsula did not run through or anywhere near Bulair, but down and across the Straits to the town of Gallipoli.' It was therefore decided to land on the toe of the peninsula, and though this spot may have been the lesser of two evils, it offered an all but insuperable disadvantage – namely, now that the Turks were roused, the British forces would have to advance up a defile, a pass flanked not by mountains but by the sea.

The strength of the force to be employed in this most difficult operation was as follows:

	Ships	Personnel	Animals	Vehicles
29th Division (Alexandria)	15	17,649	3,962	692
Anzac (Alexandria)	30	25,784	6,920	1,271
Anzac (Mudros)	5	4,854	698	147
French Forces (Alexandria)	22	16,762	3,511	647
R.N.D. (Port Said)	12	10,007	1,390	347
	84	75,056	16,481	3,104

Turning to the enemy, between March 18th and April 25th, when the first British landing took place, the Turks were given ample time wherein to entrench and prepare the more likely beaches against invasion. Yet only on March 26th was Marshal Liman von Sanders, an exceptionally capable German officer and as we shall see a born leader of men, appointed Commander-in-Chief of the Turkish forces in the peninsula; and that day he landed at Gallipoli and took over his command. Finding his troops strung out 'en cordon', he formed them into three groups: 'The 5th and 7th Divisions were stationed on the upper Saros (Xeros) Gulf; the 9th and newly organised 19th Divisions were ordered to the southern part of the peninsula; and the 11th Division was stationed on the Asiatic side, together with the 3rd, which soon arrived by boat.' Though his men were miserably enough equipped, they possessed ample rifle ammunition, but not a single aeroplane. Nevertheless, he appreciated their fighting value, which the British did not, having forgotten Plevna and its lessons. Of them General Kannengiesser writes:

'The Turkish soldier, the 'Askar,' was the Anatolian and Thracian, slightly educated, brave, trustworthy... Content with little, it never entered into his mind to dispute the authority of those above him. He followed his leader without question... The Turks are glad to feel an energetic leader's will, they feel supported in the consciousness that they are being led by a strong hand against a definite objective.'

Though the ultimate object of the campaign was the occupation of Constantinople, the immediate object was the forcing of the Narrows between Kilid Bahr on the European side of the Dardanelles and the Chanak on the Asiatic. Here the strait shrinks to 1,600 yards in width, and it was a little north of this waist, at Nagara (Abydos), where the current is not so strong, that, in 480 BC, Xerxes built his bridge, Alexander crossed in 334 BC, Barbarossa in 1190 and Orkhan in 1354. Also it was here that Hero swam the Hellespont, as centuries later also did Lord Byron.

On the western flank of this narrow strip of water lies the Gallipoli peninsula. At Bulair in the north it is no more than 4,600 yards in breadth, then it widens out to about twelve miles between Suvla Point to a little north of Akbash, narrows again to four and a half miles between Gaba Tepe and Maidos, widens once more and finally tapers off to Cape Helles. Most of this tongue of land is hilly and broken, cut up by sharp valleys, cliffs and ravines which end in the eminence of Achi Baba 700 feet above sea–level.

When war was declared the sole fortifications were at Bulair, at the entrance to the Dardanelles and at the Narrows, the last two being defended by over 100 guns, of which only fourteen were modern, and all were short of ammunition. The forts Kilid Bahr and Chanak dated from the reign of Mohammed II, who built them in 1452, and built them so well that, during the bombardment of March 18th, the 15-inch shells of the *Queen Elizabeth* did them little damage. Of roads there was but one, that running from Gallipoli to Maidos; consequently the main communications with Constantinople were by sea, a journey of about twelve hours.

Such in brief was the theatre of war, and from it I will now turn to Sir Ian Hamilton and his task, surely one of the most perplexing since Burgoyne's campaign of Saratoga.

Besides the British Mediterranean Expeditionary Force, he had under his command the French Corps Expeditionnaire d'Orient, roughly a division, commanded by General d'Amade. His plan was, whilst feinting at Bulair and Kum Kale, (1) to effect landings on Cape Helles at five points, from east to west beach 'S' in Morto Bay, 'V' and 'W' on each flank of Cape Helles and 'X' and 'Y' on its western shore; (2) simultaneously to land another force just north of Gaba Tepe, the object of which was to advance on Maidos and take in rear such Turkish forces as might oppose the Helles landings.

The plan was an able one, but, as always, its success depended upon its execution, which demanded the highest leadership and audacity. Had these been forthcoming, in my opinion, the operation might have proved successful, for today we know that the Turkish garrisons were insignificant. On April 25th, when the landings took place, south of Achi Baba there were but two infantry battalions and one company of engineers, at 'Y' beach not a man, at 'W' and 'V' two companies, at 'S' one platoon and at 'X' twelve men. Further, only 'W' and 'V' were protected by wire and machine-guns.

Unfortunately, though courage was conspicuous, true leadership was not. At 'W' and 'V' beaches disastrous delays occurred, because the landing party at 'X' was too weak. At 'V' disembarkation from SS *River Clyde,* which had been grounded, was so fiercly opposed that the landing was held up until the 26th. At 'Y', where 2,000 men stepped ashore without a shot being fired, and where for eleven hours they remained undisturbed, a complete muddle took place. Instead of advancing on Krithia unopposed they re-embarked and withdrew.

Meanwhile, the Australians and New Zealanders landed north of Gaba Tepe, one mile north of the selected beach, at a spot later to be named Anzac Cove. Their landing came as a complete surprise, and a penetration of three and a half miles was made to a spot from where the gleaming Narrows could be seen, actually the nearest point reached to them 'by any allied soldier during the campaign.' Then they were attacked by Mustafa Kemal, 'that Man of Destiny,' and driven back in such disorder that General Birdwood suggested a complete withdrawal; a request very rightly refused by Sir Ian, who replied: 'You have got through the difficult business. Now you only have to dig, dig, dig until you are safe.' Ominous words, for digging meant that surprise was over and that the whole operation had failed. Thus the foundations of one of the greatest tragedies in British history were scraped into the stony soil of the Gallipoli peninsula, close by where Alexander set out to conquer the Oriental world.

The landing having succeeded, though its object had not been attained, the second phase of the invasion was entered, a phase of wasteful frontal attacks, as hopeless and costly as any seen on the Western front. At Anzac, where the total area held measured barely 400 acres, no offensive was attempted until August 6; but at Helles three costly battles, based largely on the unwarranted optimism of General Hunter-Weston, commander of the 29th Division and GOC of the troops in the Helles area, were fought – namely, the first, second and third battles of Krithia.

The first of these, waged between April 27th and 30th, was badly conceived, and ended in chaos and a loss of some 3,000 officers and men. This failure was followed by a determined Turkish attack on May 1st. It was beaten back, and, in turn, on May 6th-7th was followed by the second battle of Krithia, of which Ashmead-Bartlett, an eye-witness, writes:

'I doubt whether, even at Leipsic, so many different nationalities have been brought together on the same battlefield. Side by side in the Anglo-French Army there fought English, Scottish and Irish regiments, Australians, New Zealanders, Sikhs, Punjabis, and Gurkhas, whilst our Navy was represented by the Naval Division and Marines.

On the other side of the Krithia road, in the French ranks, were drawn up Frenchmen, Algerians, Zouaves, Goumiers, Senegalese, and the heterogenous elements which make up the Foreign Legion.'

On the 8th the battle ended like the first of its name, but this time the casualties numbered 6,500, about 30 per cent of the numbers engaged. Next, on the 19th, the Turks attacked again, this time against Anzac, and lost 10,000 men, the Australian and New Zealand casualties numbering only 600. Then, lastly, followed the third battle of Krithia. Covered by the fire of 78 guns, supplemented, as in all these attacks, by the guns of the fleet, the 8th Corps advanced and once again was decimated, losing 4,500 officers and men out of 16,000 engaged, whilst the French lost 2,000. In the 2nd Naval Brigade 60 officers out of 70 became casualties and over 1,000 men out of 1,900. The objective of all these attacks was Achi Baba, because it was supposed to dominate the Narrows, which as a matter of fact it did not, as was discovered by Captain Keyes, Commodore to de Robeck, after the war. Then, bled white, the military operations came to a standstill.

Meanwhile, the day after the first landing took place Italy renounced the Triple Alliance and, in accordance with the Treaty of London, threw in her lot with the Allied Powers. On May 21st she was at war with Austria, whilst Mackensen fell upon the Russians along the Dunajec and drove them in rout eastwards. Then, on June 2nd, Sir Ian Hamilton telegraphed Lord Kitchener saying that 'the movement of a quarter of a million men against us seems to be well under way.' This sent a shudder through the Government, when, on the 7th, the newly constituted Dardanelles Committee was assembled to consider three alternatives – to leave things as they were, to abandon the enterprise and evacuate the peninsula, or to send out large reinforcements. Under pressure of Lord Kitchener and Mr Churchill the third course was adopted, and eventually it was decided to despatch five new divisions, Mr Churchill suggesting that they should be used to occupy the Bulair isthmus. This suggestion, however, was turned down, because Admiral de Robeck considered the threat of German submarines in the Gulf of Saros too great a risk to run.

General Birdwood was also against a landing so far north; instead he favoured a big attack from Anzac, where conditions were such as to persuade anyone to fight. Of them the official historian, an eye-witness, writes:

'The heat of the noonday sun was intense; and there was little or no shade; and the scanty water supply in the trenches was rarely sufficient for men with a parching thirst. The sickening smell of unburied corpses in No Man's Land pervaded the front areas; dense clouds of infected dust were incessant; and despite the preventive care of the doctors there was such a loathsome plague of huge flies (known to the troops as 'corpse-flies') that it was difficult to eat a mouthful of food without swallowing the pests. A tin of beef or jam, as soon as opened, would be covered with a thick film of flies, and amongst the troops in the trenches small pieces of veiling, to throw over their faces at meal times or when trying to sleep, were almost beyond price.'

The reinforcement of five divisions having been decided upon, it was agreed to organise three as a new corps, the 9th; whereupon Sir Ian Hamilton requested that either General Byng or General Rawlinson, both able officers then serving in France, should be given command. This was not agreed to, because both were junior to General Mahon, the Commander of the 10th Division of the 9th Corps; so, instead, Lieutenant-General the Hon. Sir Frederick Stopford was selected, and no worse choice could have been made. He was sixty-one years old, kindly, affable and incompetent, and during the war in South Africa had served as Military Secretary to Sir Redvers Buller. He had never commanded troops and at this time was a sick man.

Whilst these arrangements were in hand, General Hamilton, instead of conserving the energies of his army, launched three wasteful attacks – on June 21st, June 28th and July 12th-13th – in the Helles area. In these he lost 7,700 British and 4,600 French officers and men – that is, approxiamtely the effective strength of an entire division. Such generalship is hard to understand in spite of the official historian's apologies.

Once the above reinforcements were promised General Hamilton set about to consider his plan. First, it was obvious to him that the Anzac Cove area was too restricted in breadth and depth to allow of five new divisions being deployed there. Therefore, in order to gain more room, he determined to extend his base of operations by landing a force at Suvla Bay, which lay five miles to the north of the Australians and New Zealanders, and simultaneously launch two closely affiliated attacks, the object of which was the occupation of the high ground from Ejelmar Bay to Koja Chemen Tepe and thence to Baba Tepe.

This plan was an able one, for not only was it known that the Suvla area was lightly defended, but that should the Turks be surprised only four miles of open plain would have to be crossed in order to seize the surrounding hills: to the north-east the Tekke Tepe, 900 feet above sea level; to the east Anafarta Spur, 350 feet; and to the north the Kiretch Tepe, 650 feet. Could these heights be occupied within twenty-four hours, the right flank of the Turkish forces opposing the Anzac Corps would be turned, which threat would almost certainly enable General Birdwood to occupy Koja Chemen Tepe (Hill 971), the true key to the Narrows.

For this dual attack Sir Ian had at his disposal two corps,

the Australian and New Zealand and the 9th. The first consisted of the 1st and 2nd Australian Divisions and the New Zealand and Australian Division, and the second of the 10th, 11th, 13th, 53rd and 54th Divisions, the last two attached. Further, in the Helles area he had the 8th Corps, consisting of the 29th, 42nd, 52nd and the Royal Naval Divisions, as well as the Corps Expeditionnaire d'Orient – now two divisions. In all thirteen divisions. Selecting Mudros, Imbros and Mitylene as his advanced bases, he established his GHQ on the second of these islands.

Fixing on August 6th, because it was a moonless night, as the day of attack, he decided on the following operations:

Whilst the 8th Corps held by attack the Turkish forces opposing it, General Birdwood was first to feint at Lone Pine in order to draw his enemy away from the Sari Bair heights, and then assault them and carry Hill 971, Hill Q and Chunuk Bair, all three of which were to be occupied by dawn on the 7th. For these attacks the 13th Division was added to the Anzac Corps.

To land the 11th and 10th Divisions during the night of the 6th-7th south of Nibrunesi Point; the first to occupy Lala Baba, Suvla Point and Kiretch Tepe, as well as Chocolate and W Hills and Tekke Tepe (all to be gained by daylight on the 7th), whilst two brigades of the 10th Division were to advance at dawn on the 7th and make straight for the Anafarta gap in order to threaten the right rear of the Turks about Hill 971.

This plan was radically a faulty one. First, the Anzac Corps was physically worn out and the area its men would have to fight their way over was indescribably difficult. Secondly, the 10th and 11th Divisions were but half trained and the country was covered with scrub. Only the most highly trained light infantry led by the most audacious officers could have carried out a succesful overnight advance over such country. Such men and such officers Sir Ian Hamilton did not possess, therefore his plan, however brilliantly conceived, was a gamble, for requirements must fit conceptions if execution is to succeed.

Not until July 22nd was General Stopford informed of this plan, when it was impressed upon him that Chocolate and W Hills 'should be captured by a "coup de main"' before daylight,' also that bold and vigorous leadership was imperative. At first accepting it, soon he began to doubt it, possibly because General Mahon quite rightly considered it too intricate. Thereupon he pointed out his deficiency in artillery, and finding that all his troops were to be landed at 'A', 'B' and 'C' beaches, which were situated south of Nibrunesi Point, against naval advice he persuaded General Hamilton to shift 'A' to within the Bay and immediately north of the Cut. This was the first error, as we shall see.

The second must be attributed to Sir Ian himself – namely, secrecy run mad. No units had any idea of what was required of them; maps were not handed out until the evening of the 6th... 'No one except the General and Admirals knew our destination.' Physically and mentally it was a plunge into the dark, and thus 'in excelsis' a night operation.

The landing arrangements were carefully worked out, including the carriage of 400 tons of water, but these preparations seem so completely to have monopolised the attention of Stopford and his Staff and the landing itself, and not the advance from the beaches, so dominated their minds that the importance of capturing Chocolate and W Hills was lost sight of. This was also true of Sir Ian Hamilton, for in his final instructions issued to the 9th Corps on July 29 we read:

> 'Your *primary objective* will be to secure Suvla Bay... Should, however, you find it possible to achieve this object with only a portion of your force, your next step will be to give such direct assistance as is in your power to the General Officer commanding Anzac in his attack on Hill 305 [Hill 971],

by an advance on Biyuk Anafarta... He, however, directs your special attention to the fact that the Hills Yilghin [Chocolate] and Ismail Oglu Tepe [Green] are known to contain guns which can bring fire to bear on the flank and rear of an attack on Hill 305... If, therefore, it is possible *without prejudice to the attainment of your primary objective* to gain possession of those hills at an early period of your attack it will greatly facilitate the capture and retention of Hill 305.'

This watering down of the plan by making the landing the objective was the third error and the root cause of the eventual disaster, for the landing itself was but a means and not the end.

The fourth error was that Stopford, having no conception of what generalship demanded, instead of landing with his troops and establishing his headquarters on shore, decided to maintain them on board the *Jonquil,* where, incidentally, he remained throughout the 7th!

If Sir Ian Hamilton's problem was a difficult one, and it certainly was, Liman van Sanders' was out of all proportion more so. Though always afraid of a landing at Bulair, he nevertheless suspected that the British object was to occupy Koja Chemen Tepe, and that therefore a landing at Suvla Bay was possible. Equally possible was a landing south of Gaba Tepe, where he sent the 9th Division under Colonel Kannengiesser. In August his distribution was as follows: Kum Kale, 3 divisions; Bulair, 3; Anzac front, 3, under Essad Pasha; south of Gaba Tepe, 2; and in the Helles area, 5. To Suvla he sent a small body of troops known as the Anafarta Detachment. It was commanded by a Bavarian officer, Major Willmer, and it consisted of three battalions, one pioneer company, one squadron of cavalry, nineteen guns and a labour battalion. An exceptionally able officer, Willmer at once saw that his detachment was too weak to repulse a landing; all he could hope to do was to delay an invader for thirty-six to forty-eight hours from gaining the Anafarta spur, after which interval of time he might expect to be reinforced. Throwing out a forward screen of posts he held the following localities:

Kiretch Tepe, 2 companies Gallipoli Gendarmerie.

Hill 10, 3 companies Broussa Gendarmerie.

Chocolate and Green Hills, 3 companies 1/31st Regiment.

Lola Baba, 1 company 1/31st Regiment with a sentry post on Nibrunesi Point.

His reserve he placed at Baka Baba – W Hills, astride the track leading from the Bay to Anafarta Sagir.

In all he had some 1,500 men wherewith to face his enemy's 25,000.

At 2.30 p.m. on the 6th the battle, which was to decide the campaign and much more besides, opened on the Helles front, but instead of carrying out a holding attack as ordered the 8th Corps Commander foolishly attempted to capture Krithia and Achi Baba. He failed to do so at a cost of 3,500 men out of the 4,000 who attacked.

Two hours later the Anzac battle opened by an attack on the Turkish position on Lone Pine. Though successful, it led to an unfortunate event, for frightening Essad Pasha, he called to his support two regiments of Kannengiesser's 9th Division, which on arrival were well placed to reinforce Chunuk Bair when it was attacked next morning.

Directly Turkish attention was concentrated on Lone Pine, two columns of troops under Generals Johnston and Cox moved through the night, for it was 7.30 p m, to seize the Sari Bair ridge from Hill 971 to Battleship Hill. The plan of operations was complicated and impossible. Concerning this attack Ashmead-Bartlett writes:

> 'It was launched against positions the like of which had never been attacked before under modern conditions of warfare. The men were expected to climb mountains during

the night over unexplored ground, so tortuous, broken and scrubby that, had the advance taken place during peace manoeuvres, it would have been an extremely arduous task for troops to reach the summit of the Sari Bair Ridge in the prescribed time.'

The right column (Johnston's) set out obscured by the shadows cast by the ships' searchlights and moved on Table Top to gain Chunuk Bair by dawn. Part lost its way and the remainder was thrown into confusion. Meanwhile the left column (Cox's) moved up the coast and swinging right set out to gain Hill 971 and Hill Q. It took the wrong track, was sniped and delayed, the men becoming utterly exhausted. Thus the entire initial operations ended in a complete fiasco, costing 650 officers and men out of the 1,250 engaged.

Whilst these mistakes were taking place, at 5.30 a.m. on the 7th, hearing that British troops were establishing themselves on Rhododendron Spur, immediately west of Chunuk Bair, Mustafa Kemal, once again at the critical spot, called up his reserve division – the 19th – and ordered it to occupy the main ridge. Simultaneously Kannengiesser's two regiments were sent by Essad Pasha to hold this same ridge from Chunuk Bair to Hill 971. Hurrying forward with a patrol, Kannengiesser reached Chunuk Bair at about 7 a.m.

Meanwhile Liman von Sanders, realising that the hour of crisis had struck, yet ever fearful that the main blow would be directed against Bulair, telegraphed Feizi Bay, in command there, to be vigilant, and then, realising that Sari Bair must be reinforced, at 1.30 a.m. he ordered him at all possible speed to despatch three battalions south. Meanwhile the right column shook itself into some order, and at 10.40 a.m. on the 7th, about seven hours later, sent forward five companies to attack Chunuk Bair under cover of a land and sea bombardment; but almost immediately fire was opened on them by Kannengiesser's men and the attack collapsed.

This and the fact that the left column was too exhausted to accomplish anything persuaded General Godley, in command of this operation, to call off the attack until the 8th, when General Johnston was to occupy Chunuk Bair and General Cox Hill Q and Hill 971.

In all Cox's force consisted of thirteen battalions, which he divided into four columns, the objectives of which were:

1st Column, Northern slopes of Chunk Bair.
2nd Column, Southern peak of Hill Q.
3rd Column, Northern peak of Hill Q.
4th Column, Abdul Rahman spur and Hill 971.

Whilst the fourth advanced at 3 a.m. and was almost instantly checked, and the third and first were too scattered to advance, the second moved forward to link up with the 1/6th Gurkhas, who had occupied a position far out to its front; nevertheless, its men were too exhausted to reach them. Waiting in vain for their arrival, Major C J L Allanson, OC 1/6th Gurkhas, at length determined to attack Hill Q on his own, and after a fierce fight he gained a lodgment 100 feet below its crest and there he dug in, when at 2 p.m. General Godley, knowing nothing about this fine advance, suspended operations until the following day.

Meanwhile Johnston ordered an advance at 3.30 a.m., which, though it started late, to his surprise met with no opposition and so the top of the ridge was gained; whereupon Lieutenant-Colonel W G Malone, with two companies of the Wellington Battalion, started to dig in. 'The men were in high spirits. Away on their right the growing daylight was showing up the paths and tracks in rear of the enemy's lines at Anzac, now at last out-flanked. Straight to their front were the shining waters of the Narrows – the goal of the expedition. Victory seemed very near.'

Why the Turks had abandoned Chunuk Bair is not known; but as they were still holding firm on Battleship Hill and Hill Q, when dawn broke a devastating fire was opened on the flanks of Malone's small force. 'Fighting grimly, the two Wellington companies on top of the ridge maintained their exposed positions till every man was killed,' and amongst them their gallant leader. Thus Chunuk Bair was lost because Hill Q had not been taken.

For the 9th General Godley determined to renew the attack. Abandoning all idea of occupying Hill 971, he limited his objective to the main ridge from Chunuk Bair to Hill Q; Johnston to assault the former and Cox the latter, whilst in between these two vital points General A.H. Baldwin, in command of the 38th Brigade of the 13th Division, was to attack. All three forces were to work in close co-operation.

As night fell Baldwin advanced along an unreconnoitred track. Long halts and delays occurred, confusion set in and the track ending in a precipice the advance was counter-marched. As this muddle was taking place, Johnston's forward troops became heavily engaged, and as Baldwin did not appear his attack on Chunuk Bair was abandoned. Meanwhile Allanson's reinforcements having gone astray, once again he attacked on his own, and directly the bombardment lifted he gained the top of the crest, when a second bombardment started and this time fell upon his small force and drove it to its original position. Here I will let him speak for himself:

'The roar of the artillery preparation was enormous; the hill, which was almost perpendicular, seemed to leap underneath one. I recognised if we flew up the hill the moment it stopped we ought to get to the top. I put the three companies into the trenches alongside my men, and said that the moment they saw me go forward carrying a red flag, everyone was to start. I had my watch out, 5.15. I never saw such artillery preparation; the trenches were being torn to pieces, the accuracy was marvellous, as we were only just below. At 5.18 it had not stopped, and I wondered if my watch was wrong. 5.20 silence; I waited three minutes to be certain, great as the risk was. Then off we dashed, all hand in hand, a most perfect advance and a wonderful sight... At the top we met the Turks; Le Marchand was down, a bayonet through the heart. I got one through my leg, and then for about what appeared ten minutes we fought hand to hand, we bit and fisted, and used rifles and pistols as clubs, and then the Turks turned and fled, and I felt a very proud man; the key of the whole peninsular was ours, and our losses had not been so very great for such a result. Below I saw the Straits, motors and wheeled transport on the roads leading to Achi Baba. As I looked round I saw we were not being supported, and thought I could help best by going after those (Turks) who had retreated in front of us. We dashed down towards Maidos, but had only got about 100 feet down when suddenly our own Navy put six 12in. monitor shells into us; and all was terrible confusion. It was a deplorable disaster; we were obviously mistaken for Turks, and we had to get back. It was an appalling sight; the first hit a Gurkha in the face; the place was a mass of blood and limbs and screams, and we all flew back to the summit and to our old positions just below.'

Thus ended the battle for the Sari Bair ridge, a battle of valour run waste and of muddle rivalled only by the landing at Suvla Bay, to which I will now turn.

This operation, as Liman von Sanders says, was 'the political-military summit of the campaign,' yet, unlike Sari Bair, it was a feasible operation faced by no insuperable obstacles; nevertheless, like it, it was ruined by indifferent leadership and rawness of followership. 'Since the Argive host set sail for the Trojan shore no stranger collection of ships can ever have crossed the Aegean than that which converged on Suvla on the night of the 6th August, 1915.' So writes the official historian; yet to me it seems that its nearest approach in British history is Burgoyne's voyage up Lake Champlain.

At 9.30 p.m. the 32nd and 33rd Brigades of the 11th Division (General F. Hammersley) in pitch darkness approached 'B' beach to find it undefended. By 10 p.m. four battalions landed without a man being killed; yet dog-tired, for the men had been on their feet for seventeen hours. Lala Baba was occupied and the way opened to the capture of Hill 10; but no one knowing exactly where it was, nothing was done. Meanwhile the 34th Brigade, under General W.H. Sitwell, entered Suvla Bay; but, as the lighters headed for 'A' beach, when fifty feet from the shore they struck a reef, which so delayed the landing that dawn broke before the men could disembark. To make matters worse, the 10th Division (General Sir B.T. Mahon), which should have landed at 'A' beach in order to occupy Kiretch Tepe, was in part disembarked on 'C' beach and on a new one discovered north of 'A'. Thus its organisation was broken up, when complete confusion set in.

Orders and counter-orders now followed each other in rapid succession, whilst the Turkish sharpshooters, like the American riflemen of 1777, picked off the invaders by scores, and thus the situation remained from hour to hour. Not until daylight was fading did an attack on Chocolate Hill begin to develop, and as darkness set in it was carried as well as the eastern half of Green Hill. Meanwhile on the left little was done outside gaining a foothold on Kiretch Tepe. All the encircling hills remained in Turkish hands, yet more than half the 9th Corps, twenty-two battalions in all, had not been engaged; nevertheless, those which had had lost 100 officers and 1,600 men 'or rather more than the total strength of the Turks arrayed against them.'

By now not only had the whole military plan collapsed, but also the naval, for the unloading of guns, ammunition, water, supplies, carts and transport animals was vastly delayed by the general confusion. Water, though it existed in abundance, was not found; and the men having emptied their water bottles, many went nearly mad with thirst. Mobs of them collected on the beaches and were 'sucking water through holes they had made in the hoses with their bayonets.'

Of the landing, as seen by the Turks, Kannengiesser writes:

'Suvla Bay lay full of ships. We counted ten transports, six warships, and seven hospital ships. On land we saw a confused mass of troops like a disturbed ant-heap... Nowhere was there fighting in progress.'

Throughout August 7th 'General Headquarters exercised no influence over the course of the Suvla operations, and their inactivity on this day, which, in the light of after events, may be regarded as one of the crises of the World War, can only be explained as the result of over-confidence.' Hearing that even Hill 10 had not been captured, why did Sir Ian Hamilton not at once proceed to Suvla? 'Had he done so, and insisted upon immediate advance, the duration of the World War might have been very considerably shortened.' As the Commander-in-Chief sat on his island fretting for news, General Stopford sat on his ship vastly pleased that his men had got on shore. A visit to him nearly drove Commodore Keyes 'to open mutiny.' Both waited for victory or defeat as if the whole operation were a horse race. Such generalship defies definition; yet it was all part and parcel of the Moltke Staff theory that Generals-in-Chief cease to command the moment they are most needed – that is, when battle begins.

Whilst Sir Ian Hamilton and Sir Frederick Stopford were still waiting for their telephone bells to ring, all was activity on the Turkish side. At 6 p.m., Willmer telegraphed Liman von Sanders that the enemy, covered by numerous warships, had landed at Nibrunesi Point. Thereupon the Turkish Commander-in-Chief, making up his mind that Bulair was safe and that his enemy's objectives were Hill 971 and Chunuk, forthwith instructed Feizi Bey to lead two of his three divisions – namely, the 7th and 12th – south. At the same time he ordered every available man on the Asiatic side of the Dardanelles to march on Chanak and cross into Europe. Also he ordered the 8th Division from Krithia to move north. His anxiety was great, because none of these reinforcements could reach him under thirty-six to forty-eight hours. Meanwhile, could Willmer's minute force hold back the invasion? – that was the problem. Definitely the answer appeared to be 'No!' Then came a morsel of relief; at 7 p.m., Major Willmer reported: 'The landing of hostile forces has continued all day. Estimate their present strength as at least 1 1/2 divisions. No energetic attacks on the enemy's part have taken place. On the contrary, the enemy is advancing timidly.' This anyhow meant a probable gain of twenty-four hours.

At 1 a.m., on the 8th, Willmer's command was disposed as follows: Three companies of Gallipoli Gendarmerie on the Kiretch Tepe ridge; 1,100 men and five mountain guns between south of Baka Baba to W Hill, and two batteries on the eastern side of the Tekke Tepe ridge. His nearest reinforcements were the three battalions from Bulair, then dead beat and bivouacked two miles east of Turshun Kevi.

The 8th, that most critical day in the whole campaign, was a Sunday, and so far as the 9th Corps was concerned it was to be a day of rest, and so completely out of touch was the British Commander-in-Chief that, at 10.50 a.m., he sent Stopford the following message: 'You and your troops have indeed done splendidly. Please tell Hammerseley how much we hope from his able and rapid advance.'

'Splendid' and 'rapid'! Why, outside the muddled landing

itself practically nothing had been accomplished, and, worse still, Stopford was incapable of accomplishing anything; for as the official historian writes: As on the 7th 'the basic cause' of inaction on the 8th 'was the absence of a resolute leadership, not only on shore but at corps headquarters and even at GHQ.' Then he continues:

> 'Following a quiet night, the morning of the 8th was absolutely still. Out of a cloudless sky, the sun was shining fiercely. The enemy's guns were silent. Apart from an occasional rifle-shot on Kiretch Tepe there was not a sound of war. The sand-dunes near the Cut were crowded with resting troops. The shores of the bay were fringed with naked figures bathing. General Stopford and his chief staff officer were still on board *Jonquil,* and had not yet been ashore.'

As no news was received at GHQ, it was decided to send Colonel Aspinall (later on the official historian) ashore to ascertain what was taking place. At 9.30 a.m. he set out, and found the whole bay at peace. Arriving on board *Jonquil* he met General Stopford, who was 'in excellent spirits'... 'Well, Aspinall,' he said, 'the men have done splendidly, and have been magnificent.' 'But they haven't reached the hills,' replied Aspinall. 'No,' answered Stopford, 'but they are ashore.' Thereupon Aspinall sent the following wireless message to GHQ: 'Just been ashore, where I found all quiet. No rifle fire, no artillery fire, and apparently no Turks. 9th Corps resting. Feel confident that golden opportunities are being lost and look upon the situation as serious.'

Whilst Aspinall was ashore, news was received at GHQ that Turkish troops were advancing east of Tekke Tepe, whereupon Stopford was urged to push on. Transmitting this information to his divisional commanders, he added to it that 'in view of want of adequate artillery support I do not want you to attack an entrenched position held in strength' – so nothing was done.

At length Sir Ian himself decided to go ashore, which he was unable to do until 4.30 p.m., because his destroyer was having her fires drawn! Proceeding first to the *Jonquil,* he found Stopford 'happy', for in that General's opinion 'everything was quite all right and going well.' Further, he informed him that 'he had decided to postpone the occupation of the ridge [Kiretch Tepe] (which might lead to a regular battle) until next morning.' Then writes Sir Ian: "A regular battle is just exactly what we are here for" was what I was inclined to say; but did not.' Then he decided to visit Hammersley's headquarters; whereupon Stopford asked to be excused from accompanying him... 'he had not been very fit; he had just returned from a visit to the shore [400 yards away] and he wanted to give his leg a chance.'

At Hammersley's headquarters General Hamilton found reigning a chaotic peace. 'Here,' he writes, 'was a victorious division, rested and watered, said to be unable to bestir itself, even feebly, with less than twelve hours' notice! This was what I felt, and although I did not say it probably I looked it.' Thereupon he ordered an immediate attack on the Tekke Tepe ridge, which resulted in looking for units, finding them, marching them and counter-marching them; during which turmoil the first Turkish reinforcements from Bulair, dead beat, occupied the crest of the ridge. Thus all surprise vanished; from now on equal forces were to face each other in the field.

'During the whole of 8th August,' writes Kannengiesser, 'the goddess of victory held the door to success wide open for Stopford, but he would not enter... But nobody advanced. In short, a peaceful picture, almost like a boy scouts' field day.'

'At the same time under the same sun on the other side of the painting troops of the 7th and 12th Divisions were straining forward over the hills from Bulair; from the Asiatic side along the shadeless Sultan's Way; over Erenkoi the Turkish battalions and batteries were pressing towards the embarkation stations in Tchanak Kale [Chanak]. Will they arrive in time? This thought feverishly occupied the mind... of the Marshal who waited there by Anafarta.'

Whilst the British Commander-in-Chief was looking ferocious and thinking what he was inclined to say and yet remaining dumb, Marshal Liman von Sanders was all fire and activity. Before daybreak he mounted his horse, searched for his reinforcements and found the Staff Officer of the 7th Division, who informed him that both it and the 12th were still far behind. Anxiously he looked over the battlefield at the invading horde. Between it and where he stood were 400 men on W Hills, 300 on Kiretch Tepe, and not a man in between. That evening he heard from Willmer that Feizi Bey had not arrived. He summoned him to him, and when that General told him that his troops were too exhausted to attack before the morning of the 9th, what did he do? Being no drawing-room General he dismissed him on the spot and placed Mustafa Kamel Bey in command of all troops in the Anafarta section, because, as he says, 'he was a leader that delighted in responsibility.'

As August 7th and 8th were days of crisis, so were the 9th and 10th days of decision. After a series of orders and counter-orders, Hammersley was instructed to carry the Anafarta spur at 5 a.m. on the 9th, and Mahon to occupy Tekke Tepe. The attack of the 11th Division opened in confusion and ended in chaos. As the leading battalion of the 32nd Brigade moved forward, Turkish reinforcements were pouring up the other side of the ridge, then a clash took place and the battalion was thrown back in confusion. 'Despite the 48 hours' delay, the race for Tekke Tepe' was 'lost by rather less than half an hour.'

The attack of the 33rd Brigade was only a little less chaotic. As it advanced it was met by crowds of stragglers flatulent with stories of defeat. Then it met the Turks at Asmak Dere, was stopped, held its own and dug in. Meanwhile at Kiretch Tepe a short advance was made, when the attackers of the 10th Division also dug in as did General Stopford, who had now established his headquarters ashore. 'Walking up the lower slope of Kiretch Tepe Sirt,' writes Sir Ian Hamilton, 'we found Stopford, about four or five hundred yards east of Ghazi Baba, busy with a part of a Field Company of Engineers supervising the building of some splinter-proof Headquarters huts for himself and Staff. He was absorbed in the work, and he said that it would probably be well to make a thorough good job of the dug-outs as we should probably be here for a very long time.'

Next day the 53rd Division (now landed) was thrown into the battle to retake Scimitar Hill, lost on the 9th, and to assault the Anafarta Spur. Two attacks were made, and both failed.

Commenting on these two days' fighting, Ashmead-Bartlett writes:

'No one seemed to know where the headquarters of the different brigades and divisions were to be found. The troops were hunting for water, the staffs were hunting for their troops, and the Turkish snipers were hunting for their prey... Where I had seen one Turk yesterday there seemed to be ten to-day... Leaving comparatively few in the trenches, large numbers descended into the unburnt scrub, and there, almost immune from artillery fire, awaited our attack... Their snipers crept from bush to bush, from tree to tree, from knoll to knoll, picking off our men wherever they saw a favourable target, and were themselves left almost unmolested.'

Indeed, it was Saratoga over again.

This day Mustafa Kamel Bey also attacked. Having on the 9th checked the 9th Corps, on the 10th he turned on Chunuk

Bair, and having personally reconnoitred that position, he decided to recapture Rhododendron Spur. At 4.45 a.m., dense waves of Turks poured across the skyline, and sweeping over their enemy's advanced trenches captured the Pinnacle and the Farm. Then the attack exhausted itself. Thus, on the 10th, ended the Battles of Sari Bair and Suvla Bay. What were their cost to the invader? Out of 50,000 British troops, 18,000 were killed, wounded and missing. Well may Ashmead-Bartlett jot down on the 12th: 'We have landed again and dug another graveyard.'

The remainder of this campaign must be told in brief. Stopford was dismissed and replaced by General Sir Julian Byng, who originally had been asked for. 'This is a young man's war,' now wrote Lord Kitchener, just six months too late; yet Sir Ian, as responsible for the disaster, remained on to carry out on August 21th–22nd a wasteful frontal attack at Suvla. This last battle cost 5,300 in killed, wounded and missing out of 14,300.

The immediate result of the British failure was the mobilisation of the Bulgarian Army on September 25th. Next, on October 14th, Bulgaria declared war on Serbia, whereupon Lord Kitchener decided to withdraw two divisions from the Dardanelles for service at Salonika. Then the storm burst, Mackensen at the head of nine German and Austrian divisions crossing the Danube. Uskub fell on the 22nd, Nish on November 2 and Monastir was entered on December 2, Serbia being reduced to ruin, while German guns and ammunition poured into Constantinople.

On October 14th, Sir Ian Hamilton was recalled to England to be replaced by Sir Charles Munro, who, landing on the 28th, on the 31st recommended the total evacuation of the British forces. This threw Mr Asquith into a panic, and, on November 2nd, he decided to entrust the entire conduct of the war to a War Committee of not less than three and not more than five members, a change he should have initiated a year or more before. Then, on the 4th, Lord Kitchener was sent out to the Dardanelles to give a second opinion and to get rid of him, as Asquith informed Lloyd George. In turn, he sent back a half-hearted answer that evacuation was inevitable, whereupon Mr. Churchill, long superseded by Mr Balfour as First Lord of the Admiralty, pressed for a renewal of the naval attack on the Narrows, though now its strategic purpose had vanished. In this vain attempt to spoon up spilt milk, he was strongly supported by Commodore Keyes, who rushed this idea here, there, and everywhere like a tactical bull in a strategical china shop. To him, the forcing of the Narrows meant that the 'whole business' would be finished. He could not see that Germany and Turkey were now without a dividing frontier, and that once the fleet had bombarded Constantinople nothing further could have been done. Nor did he know at the time that on the German-Turkish side ' a large-scale offensive with the assistance of gas was in course of preparation,' though this might have been guessed.

Then, on November 27th, a terrific blizzard swept the peninsula for seventy-two hours, in which hundreds of men died of exposure.' At Suvla alone in the course of the three days' storm there had been more than 5,000 cases of frost-bite, and over 200 men had been drowned or frozen to death.' This storm hastened the crisis; for though General Munro had estimated that the probable losses involved in the evacuation would total between thirty and forty percent of the personnel and material then on the peninsula, after much intrigue and wrangling the War Committee at first decided to evacuate Anzac and Suvla only, but later on Helles as well. The evacuation of the first two was carried out by December 20th, and the last by January 9th, 1915, without a single soldier killed. Thus were concluded the sole successful operations of the campaign. In all 410,000 British and 70,000 French soldiers had been landed, of whom 252,000 were killed, wounded, missing, prisoners, died of disease or evacuated sick. The Turkish casualties amounted to 218,000 men, of whom nearly 66,000 were killed. The booty left behind was immense: 'It took nearly two years to clean up the ground.'

MAJOR-GENERAL JOHN FREDERICK CHARLES FULLER

A Drink's a Drink

After the debacle on the Somme I was withdrawn from the line, for the simple reason that officialdom had somehow discovered I was too young to have been there in the first place. I was sent down to Auxi-le-Chateau and, having by now been promoted to Corporal, was put in charge of the Officers' Mess.

It was my job to see that the catering was up to scratch, but more importantly to ensure that drinks were always available. Officers were allowed whisky or whatever they fancied and received it regularly from England, a privilege naturally not extended to the Other Ranks. My problem though was to find whatever I could in the form of mineral water to add to the drinks from the French shops. This was far from easy, since the French way of drinking is far different from ours.

One evening I went to the local estaminet to find whatever I could to place on the table for splicing the drinks and, as usual, struck a dry well. However, I poked about the shelves and at last came across some dark-brown bottles which looked promising insofar as their contents were fizzy. They would obviously fit the bill, so I bought them and carried them thankfully back to the chateau. Once again the officers were in luck.

Early next morning I was taking the air in the grounds when General Gully Flood opened the French doors of the chateau and called, 'Corporal Price!'

'Sah!'

'Here.'

I doubled smartly over, stood to attention and saluted.

He eyed me coldly and said, 'Corporal, what in the name of God was that stuff we put in our whisky last night?'

'Er... I'm not sure, sir. It looked alright.'

'Well, find out' the General bawled. 'This morning we're all *pissing green!*'

I never did, of course. Couldn't speak French, could I?

DON J. PRICE

A Period on the Passchendale Ridge

After having spent eight days on rest in cellars and dug-outs in the badly-battered Ypres we were moving back up the front line. One of our lads carrying the mail was blown to pieces and our letters were scattered away in the wind. It was dark and bitterly cold. Fear was beginning to mount again – the usual dread of what the 'morrow might bring.

The earth had been churned into a sea of mud and water beneath the constant shelling and shell-holes, large and small, had totally obliterated what had once been rich vegetation. All that remained of the magnificent trees was the occasional stump, the majority of which leaned drunkenly this way and that. Very lights floating down along the ridge turned them into weird and awesome shapes. The whole place exuded evil.

We were being shelled continually and our casualties were mounting. Cries for stretcher-bearers were heard repeatedly, though the chances of rescue were dim.

We continued to make our way up, though our progress was slow and deliberate over the duckboards laid across the broken land. Heavily laden with thick overcoats, equipment, rifles, ammunition and rations as we were, falling off the duckboards could prove fatal. We were wet through and cold, and the shelling did not help, but eventually we arrived at our destination.

There was no trench. The line consisted of a series of shell-holes joined together and mostly half full of water. Two of us were allocated one which was reasonably dry. This was to be our 'home' for two days and nights. It was deep enough for us to dig a sleeping-hole in the side – assuming we ever reached a stage of resting, which was rare indeed.

Covered in lice, big fat rats were our constant companions, nosing and squeaking about and finding more than they could ever need to eat. The smell of rotting flesh and mustard gas was nauseating, though oddly one grew used to it. The bloated bodies of mules and horses littered the landscape, along with various items of equipment and dud unexploded shells. Hereabouts, the Germans were no more than 200 yards away, but as their conditions were no doubt the same as ours they kept very quiet, even moderating their shelling.

From time to time the call of nature had to be answered and as you practically had to undress, it was quite an effort. To get your trousers down and at the same time keep your head below the parapet took some doing. A moment's carelessness meant almost certain death.

Sometimes I ask myself, how was it that a boy of eighteen could live such a life and remain sane, but the human mind has its own defences. Death was so common that one passed it by with scarcely a glance. At Roll Call after an attack, 'He got one through his bloody tin hat,' was a typical laconic comment when someone was declared missing. It seems callous, but any sympathy would have seen us all into our graves.

I emerged unscathed from that period in the line, but during a similar visit I was wounded by shrapnel and a mustard gas shell, which exploded on the parapet of our trench, spraying my back. The burning was not too severe though and within weeks both ailments were cleared and I was back in the line.

I enlisted in 1914 at the age of sixteen and fought in most of the major battles, finally to be demobbed in December of 1918. For this service I was awarded the princely sum of £5.

DON J. PRICE

from *'A Farewell To Arms'* – *The Retreat from Caporetto*

At noon we were stuck in a muddy road about, as nearly as we could figure, ten kilometres from Udine. The rain had stopped during the forenoon and three times we had heard planes coming, seen them pass overhead, watched them go far to the left and heard them bombing on the main highroad. We had worked through a network of secondary roads and had taken many roads that were blind, but had always, by backing up and finding another road, gotten closer to Udine. Now, Aymo's car, in backing so that we might get out of a blind road, had gotten in to the soft earth at the side and the wheels, spinning, had dug deeper and deeper until the car rested on its differential. The thing to do now was to dig out in front of the wheels, put in brush so that the chains could grip, and then push until the car was on the road. We were all down on the road around the car. The two sergeants looked at the car and examined the wheels. Then they started off down the road without a word. I went after them.

'Come on,' I said. 'Cut some brush.'

'We have to go,' one said.

'Get busy,' I said, 'and cut brush.'

'We have to go,' one said. The other said nothing. They were in a hurry to start. They would not look at me.

'I order you to get back to the car and cut brush,' I said. The one sergeant turned. 'We have to go on. In a little while you will be cut off. You can't order us. You're not our officer.'

'I order you to cut brush,' I said. They turned and started down the road.

'Halt,' I said. They kept on down the muddy road, the hedge on either side. 'I order you to halt,' I called. They went a little faster. I opened up my holster, took the pistol, aimed at the one who had talked the most, and fired. I missed and they both started to run. I shot three times and dropped one. The other went through the hedge and was out of sight. I fired at him through the hedge as he ran across the field. The pistol clicked empty and I put in another clip. I saw it was too far to shoot at the second sergeant. He was far across the field, running, his head low. I commenced to reload the empty clip. Bonello came up.

'Let me go finish him,' he said. I handed him the pistol and he walked down to where the sergeant of engineers lay face down across the road. Bonello leaned over, put the pistol against the man's head and pulled the trigger. The pistol did not fire.

'You have to cock it,' I said. He cocked it and fired twice. He took hold of the sergeant's legs and pulled him to the side of the road so he lay beside the hedge. He came back and handed me the pistol.

'The son of a bitch,' he said. He looked toward the sergeant. 'You see me shoot him, Tenente?'

'We've got to get the brush quickly,' I said. 'Did I hit the other one at all?'

'I don't think so,' Aymo said. 'He was too far away to hit with a pistol.'

'The dirty scum,' Piani said. We were all cutting twigs and branches. Everything had been taken out of the car. Bonello was digging out in front of the wheels. When we were ready Aymo started the car and put it into gear. The wheels spun round throwing brush and mud. Bonello and I pushed until we could feel our joints crack. The car would not move.

'Rock her back and forth, Barto,' I said.

He drove the engine in reverse, then forward. The wheels only dug in deeper. Then the car was resting on the differential again, and the wheels spun freely in the holes they had dug. I straightened up.

'We'll try her with a rope,' I said.

'I don't think it's any use, Tenente. You can't get a straight pull.'

'We'll have to try it,' I said. 'She won't come out any other way.'

Piani's and Bonello's cars could only move straight ahead down the narrow road. We roped both cars together and pulled. The wheels only pulled sideways against the ruts.

'It's no good,' I shouted. 'Stop it.'

Piani and Bonello got down from their cars and came back. Aymo got down. The girls were up the road about forty yards sitting on a stone wall.

'What do you say, Tenente?' Bonello asked.

'We'll dig out and try once more with the brush,' I said. I

looked down the road. It was my fault. I had led them up here. The sun was almost out from behind the clouds and the body of the sergeant lay beside the hedge.

'We'll put his cape and coat under,' I said. Bonello went to get them. I cut brush and Aymo and Piani dug out in front and between the wheels. I cut the cape, then ripped it in two, and laid it under the wheel in the mud, then piled brush for the wheels to catch. We were ready to start and Aymo got up on the seat and started the car. The wheels spun and we pushed and pushed. But it wasn't any use.

'It's ****ed,' I said. 'Is there anything you want in the car, Barto?'

Aymo climbed up with Bonello, carrying the cheese and two bottles of wine and his cape. Bonello, sitting behind the wheel, was looking through the pockets of the sergeant's coat.

'Better throw the coat away,' I said. 'What about Barto's virgins?'

'They can get in the back,' Piani said. 'I don't think we are going far.'

I opened the back door of the ambulance.

'Come on,' I said. 'Get in.' The two girls climbed in and sat in the corner. They seemed to have taken no notice of the shooting. I looked back up the road. The sergeant lay in his dirty long-sleeved underwear. I got up with Piani and we started. We were going to try to cross the field. When the road entered the field I got down and walked ahead. If we could get across, there was a road on the other side. We could not get across. It was too soft and muddy for the cars. When they were finally and completely stalled, the wheels dug in to the hubs, we left them in the field and started on foot for Udine.

When we came to the road which led back toward the main highway I pointed down it to the two girls.

'Go down there,' I said. 'You'll meet people.' They looked

at me. I took out my pocket-book and gave them each a ten-lira note. 'Go down there,' I said, pointing. 'Friends! Family!'

They did not understand but they held the money tightly and started down the road. They looked back as though they were afraid I might take the money back. I watched them go down the road, their shawls close around them, looking back apprehensively at us. The three drivers were laughing.

'How much will you give me to go in that direction, Tenente?' Bonello asked.

'They're better off in a bunch of people than alone if they catch them,' I said.

'Give me two hundred lire and I'll walk straight back toward Austria,' Bonello said.

'They'd take it away from you,' Piani said.

'Maybe the war will be over,' Aymo said.

We were going up the road as fast as we could. The sun was trying to come through. Beside the road were mulberry trees. Through the trees I could see our two big moving-vans of cars stuck in the field. Piani looked back too.

'They'll have to build a road to get them out,' he said.

'I wish to Christ we had bicycles,' Bonello said.

'Do they ride bicycles in America?' Aymo asked.

'They used to.'

'Here it is a great thing,' Aymo said. ' A bicycle is a splendid thing.'

'I wish to Christ we had bicycles,' Bonello said. 'I'm no walker.'

'Is that firing?' I asked. I thought I could hear firing a long way away.

'I don't know,' Aymo said. He listened.

'I think so,' I said.

'The first thing we will see will be the cavalry,' Piani said.

'I don't think they've got any cavalry.'

'I hope to Christ not,' Bonello said. 'I don't want to be stuck on a lance by any ****ing cavalry.'

'You certainly shot that sergeant, Tenente,' Piani said.

We were walking fast.

'I killed him,' Bonello said. 'I never killed anybody in this war, and all my life I've wanted to kill a sergeant.'

'You killed him on the sit all right,' Piani said. 'He wasn't flying very fast when you killed him.'

'Never mind. That's one thing I can always remember. I killed that shit of a sergeant.'

'What will you say in confession?' Aymo asked.

'I'll say, "Bless me, father, I killed a sergeant."' They all laughed.

'He's an anarchist,' Piani said. 'He doesn't go to church.'

'Piani's an anarchist too,' Bonello said.

'Are you really anarchists?' I asked.

'No, Tenente. We're socialists. We come from Imola.'

'Haven't you ever been there?'

'No.'

'By Christ it's a fine place, Tenente. You come there after the war and we'll show you something.'

'Are you all socialists?'

'Everybody.'

'Is it a fine town?'

'Wonderful. You never saw a town like that.'

'How did you get to be socialists?'

'We're all socialists. Everybody is a socialist. We've always been socialists.'

'You come, Tenente. We'll make you a socialist too.'

Ahead the road turned off to the left and there was a little hill and, beyond a stone wall, an apple orchard. As the road went uphill they ceased talking. We walked along together all going fast against time.

We were on a road that led to a river. There was a long line of abandoned trucks and carts on the road leading up to the bridge. No one was in sight. The river was high and the

bridge had been blown up in the centre; the stone arch
fallen into the river and the brown water was going over it. We went up on the bank looking for a place to cross. Up ahead I knew there was a railway bridge and I thought we might be able to get across there. The path was wet and muddy. We did not see any troops; only abandoned trucks and stores. Along the river bank there was nothing and no one but the wet brush and muddy ground. We went up to the bank and finally we saw the railway bridge.

'What a beautiful bridge,' Aymo said. It was a long plain iron bridge across what was usually a dry river-bed.

'We'd better hurry and get across before they blow it up,' I said.

'There's nobody to blow it up,' Piani said. 'They're all gone.'

'It's probably mined,' Bonello said. 'You cross first, Tenente.'

'Listen to the anarchist,' Aymo said. 'Make him go first.'

'I'll go,' I said. 'It won't be mined to blow up with one man.'

'You see,' Piani said. 'That is brains. Why haven't you brains, anarchist?'

'If I had brains I wouldn't be here,' Bonello said.

'That's pretty good, Tenente,' Aymo said.

'That's pretty good,' I said. We were close to the bridge now. The sky had clouded over again and it was raining a little. The bridge looked long and solid. We climbed up the embankment.

'Come one at a time,' I said and started across the bridge. I watched the ties and rails for any trip-wires or signs of explosive but I saw nothing. Down below the gaps in the ties the river ran muddy and fast. Ahead across the wet countryside I could see Udine in the rain. Across the bridge I looked back. Just up the river was another bridge. As I watched, a yellow mud-colored motor car crossed it. The sides of the bridge were high and the body of the car, once on, was out of sight. But I saw the heads of the driver, the man on the seat with him, and the two men on the rear seat. They all wore German helmets. The car was over the bridge and out of sight behind the trees and the abandoned vehicles on the road. I waved to Aymo who was crossing and to the others to come on. I climbed down and crouched beside the railway embankment, Aymo came down with me.

'Did you see the car?' I asked.

'No. We were watching you.'

'A German staff car crossed on the upper bridge.'

'A staff car?'

'Yes.'

'Holy Mary.'

The others came and we all crouched in the mud behind the embankment, looking across the rails at the bridge, the line of trees, the ditch and the road.

'Do you think we're cut off then, Tenente?'

'I don't know. All I know is a German staff car went along that road.'

'You don't feel funny, Tenente? You haven't got strange feelings in the head?'

'Don't be funny, Bonello.'

'What about a drink?' Piani asked. 'If we're cut off we might as well have a drink.' He unhooked his canteen and uncorked it.

'Look! Look!' Aymo said and pointed toward the road. Along the top of the stone bridge we could see German helmets moving. They were bent forward and moved smoothly, almost supernaturally, along. As they came off the bridge we saw them. They were bicycle troops. I saw the faces of the first two. They were ruddy and healthy-looking. Their helmets came down low over their foreheads and the sides of their faces. Their carbines were clipped to the frame of the bicycles. Stick bombs hung handle down from their belts. Their helmets and their gray uniforms were wet and they rode easily, looking ahead and to both sides. There were two – then four in line, then two, almost a dozen; then another dozen – then one alone. They did not talk but we could not have heard them because of the noise from the river. They were gone out of sight up the road.

'Holy Mary,' Aymo said.

'They were Germans,' Piani said. 'Those weren't Austrians.'

'Why isn't there somebody here to stop them?' I said. 'Why haven't they blown the bridge up? Why aren't there machine-guns along this embankment?'

'You tell us, Tenente,' Bonello said.

I was very angry.

'The whole bloody thing is crazy. Down below they blow up a little bridge. Here they leave a bridge on the main road. Where is everybody? Don't they try and stop them at all?'

'You tell us, Tenente,' Bonello said. I shut up. It was none of my business; all that I had to do was to get to Pordenone with three ambulances. I had failed at that. All I had to do now was get to Pordenone. I probably could not even get to Udine. The hell I couldn't. The thing to do was to be calm and not get shot or captured.

'Didn't you have a canteen open?' I asked Piani. He handed it to me. I took a long drink. 'We might as well start,' I said. 'There's no hurry though. Do you want to eat something?'

'This is no place to stay,' Bonello said.

'All right. We'll start.'

'Should we keep on this side – out of sight ?'

'We'll be better off on top. They may come along this bridge too. We don't want them on top of us before we see them.'

We walked along the railroad track. On both sides of us stretched the wet plain. Ahead across the plain was the hill of Udine. The roofs fell away from the castle on the hill. We could see the campanile and the clock-tower. There were many mulberry trees in the fields. Ahead I saw a place where the rails were torn up. The ties had been dug out too and thrown down the embankment.

'Down! Down!' Aymo said. We dropped down beside the embankment. There was another group of bicycles passing along the road. I looked over the edge and saw them go on.

'They saw us but they went on,' Aymo said.

'We'll get killed up there, Tenente,' Bonello said.

'They don't want us,' I said. 'They're after something else. We're in more danger if they should come on us suddenly.'

'I'd rather walk here out of sight,' Bonello said.

'All right. We'll walk along the tracks.'

'Do you think we can get through?' Aymo asked.

'Sure. There aren't very many of them yet. We'll go through in the dark.'

'What was that staff car doing?'

'Christ knows,' I said. We kept on the tracks. Bonello tired of walking in the mud of the embankment and came up with the rest of us. The railway moved south away from the highway now and we could see what passed along the road. A short bridge over a canal was blown up but we climbed over what was left of the span. We heard firing ahead of us.

We came up on the railway beyond the canal. It went on straight toward the town across the low fields. We could see the line of the other railway ahead of us. To the north was the main road where we had seen the cyclists; to the south there was a small branch-road across the fields with thick trees on each side. I thought we had better cut to the south and work around the town that way and across country toward Campoformio and the main road to the Tagliamento. We could avoid the main line of the retreat by keeping to the secondary roads beyond Udine. I knew there were plenty of side-roads across the plain. I started down the embankment.

'Come on,' I said. We would make for the side-road and

work to the south of the town. We all started down the embankment. A shot was fired at us from the side-road. The bullet went into the mud of the embankment.

'Go on back,' I shouted. I started up the embankment, slipping in the mud. The drivers were ahead of me. I went up the embankment as fast as I could go. Two more shots came from the thick brush and Aymo, as he was crossing the tracks, lurched, tripped and fell face down. We pulled him to the side and turned him over. 'His head ought to be uphill,' I said. Piani moved him around. He lay in the mud on the side of the embankment, his feet pointing downhill, breathing blood irregularly. The three of us squatted over him in the rain. He was hit low in the back of the neck and the bullet had ranged upward and come out under the right eye. He died while I was stopping up the two holes. Piani laid his head down, wiped at his face, with a piece of emergency dressing, then let it alone.

'The shits,' he said.

'They weren't Germans,' I said. 'There can't be any Germans over there.'

'Italians,' Piani said, using the word as an epithet, 'Italiani!' Bonello said nothing. He was sitting beside Aymo, not looking at him. Piani picked up Aymo's cap where it had rolled down the embankment and out it over his face. He took out his canteen.

'Do you want a drink?' Piani handed Bonello the canteen.

'No,' Bonello said. He turned to me. 'That might have happened to us any time on the railway tracks.'

'No,' I said. 'It was because we started across the field.'

Bonello shook his head. 'Aymo's dead,' he said. 'Who's dead next, Tenente? Where do we go now?'

'Those were Italians that shot,' I said. 'They weren't Germans.'

'I suppose if they were Germans they'd have killed all of us,' Bonello said.

'We're in more danger from Italians than Germans,' I said. 'The rear guard are afraid of everything. The Germans know what they're after.'

'You reason it out, Tenente,' Bonello said.

'Where do we go now?' Piani asked.

'We'd better lie up some place till it's dark. If we could get south we'd be all right.'

'They'd have to shoot us all to prove they were right the first time,' Bonello said. 'I'm not going to try them.'

'We'll find a place to lie up as near to Udine as we can get and then go through when it's dark.'

'Let's go then,' Bonello said. We went down the north side of the embankment. I looked back. Aymo lay in the mud with the angle of the embankment. He was quite small and his arms were by his side, his puttee-wrapped legs and muddy boots together, his cap over his face. He looked very dead. It was raining. I liked him as well as anyone I ever knew. I had his papers in my pocket and would write to his family. Ahead across the fields was a farmhouse. There were trees around it and the farm buildings were built against the house. There was a balcony along the second floor held up by columns.

'We'd better keep a little way apart,' I said. 'I'll go ahead.' I started toward the farmhouse. There was a path across the field.

Crossing the field, I did not know but that some one would fire on us from the trees near the farmhouse itself. I walked toward it, seeing it very clearly. The balcony of the second floor merged into the barn and there was hay coming out between the columns. The courtyard was of stone blocks and all the trees were dripping with the rain. There was a big empty two-wheeled cart, the shafts tipped high up in the rain. The door of the house was open and I went in. Bonello and Piani came in after me. It was dark inside. I went back to the kitchen. There were ashes of a fire in the big open hearth. The pots hung over the ashes, but they were empty. I looked around but I could not find anything to eat.

'We ought to lie up in the barn,' I said. 'Do you think you could find anything to eat, Piani, and bring it up there?'

'I'll look,' Piani said.

'I'll look too,' Bonello said.

'All right,' I said. 'I'll go and look at the barn.' I found a stone stairway that went up from the stable underneath. The stable smelt dry and pleasant in the rain. The cattle were all gone, probably driven off when they left. The barn was half full of hay. There were two windows in the roof, one was blocked with boards, the other was a narrow dormer window on the north side. There was a chute so that hay might be pitched down to the cattle. Beams crossed the opening down into the main floor where the hay-carts drove in when the hay was hauled in to be pitched up. I heard the rain on the roof and smelled the hay and, when I went down, the clean smell of dried dung in the stable. We could pry a board loose and see out of the south window down into the courtyard. The other window looked out on the field toward the north. We could get out of either window onto the roof and down, or go down the hay chute if the stairs were impractical. It was a big barn and we could hide in the hay if we heard any one. It seemed like a good place. I was sure we could have gotten through to the south if they had not fired on us. It was impossible that there were Germans there. They were coming from the north and down the road from Cividale. They could not have come through from the south. The Italians were even more dangerous. They were frightened and firing on anything they saw. Last night on the retreat we had heard that there had been many Germans in Italian uniforms mixing with the retreat in the north. I did not believe it. That was one of the things you always heard in war. It was one of the things the enemy always did to you. You did not know any one who went over in German uniform to confuse them. Maybe they did but it sounded difficult. I did not believe the Germans did it. I did not believe they had to. There was no need to confuse our retreat. The size of the army and the fewness of the roads did that. Nobody gave any orders, let alone Germans. Still, they would shoot us for Germans. They shot Aymo. The hay smelled good and lying in a barn in the hay took away all the years in between. We had lain in hay and talked and shot sparrows with an air-rifle when they perched in the triangle cut high up in the wall of the barn. The barn was gone now and one year they had cut the hemlock woods and there were only stumps, dried tree-tops, branches and fireweed where the woods had been. You could not go back. If you did not go forward what happened? You never got back to Milan. And if you got back to Milan what happened? I listened to the firing to the north toward Udine. I could hear machine-gun firing. There was no shelling. That was something. They must have gotten some troops along the road. I looked down in the half-light of the hay-barn and saw Piani standing on the hauling floor. He had a long sausage, a jar of something and two bottles of wine under his arm.

'Come up,' I said. 'There is the ladder.' Then I realized that I should help him with the things and went down. I was vague in the head from lying in the hay. I had been nearly asleep.

'Where's Bonello?' I asked.

'I'll tell you,' Piani said. We went up the ladder. Up on the hay we set the things down. Piani took out his knife with the corkscrew and drew the cork on a wine bottle.

'They have sealing-wax on it,' he said. 'It must be good.' He smiled.

'Where's Bonello?' I asked.

Piani looked at me.

'He went away, Tenente,' he said. 'He wanted to be a prisoner.'

I did not say anything.

'He was afraid we would get killed.'

I held the bottle of wine and did not say anything.

'You see we don't believe in the war anyway, Tennete.'

'Why didn't you go?' I asked.

'I did not want to leave you.'

'Where did he go?'

'I don't know, Tenente. He went away.'

'All right,' I said. 'Will you cut the sausage?'

Piani looked at me in the half light.

'I cut it while we were talking,' he said. We sat in the hay and ate the sausage and drank the wine. It must have been the wine they had saved for a wedding. It was so old it was losing its colour.

'You look out of this window, Luigi,' I said. 'I'll go look out the other window.'

We had each been drinking out of one of the bottles and I took my bottle with me and went over and lay flat on the hay and looked out the narrow window at the wet country. I do not know what I expected to see but I did not see anything except the fields and the bare mulberry trees and the rain falling. I drank the wine and it did not make me feel good. They had kept it too long and it had gone to pieces and lost its quality and colour. I watched it get dark outside; the darkness came very quickly. It would be a black night with the rain. When it was dark there was no use watching any more, so I went over to Piani. He was lying asleep and I did not wake him but sat down beside him for a while. He was a big man and he slept heavily. After a while I woke him and we started.

That was a very strange night. I do not know what I had expected, death perhaps and shooting in the dark and running, but nothing happened. We waited, lying flat beyond the ditch along the main road while a German battalion passed, then when they were gone we crossed the road and went on to the north. We were very close to Germans twice in the rain but they did not see us. We got past the town to the north without seeing any Italians, then after a while came on the main channels of the retreat and walked all night toward the Tagliamento. I had not realized how gigantic the retreat was. The whole country was moving, as well as the army. We walked all night, making better time than the vehicles. My leg ached and I was tired but we made good time. It seemed so silly for Bonello to have decided to be taken prisoner. There was no danger. We had walked through two armies without incident. If Aymo had not been killed there would never have seemed to be any danger. No one had bothered us when we were in plain sight along the railway. The killing came suddenly and unreasonably. I wondered where Bonello was.

'How do you feel, Tenente?' Piani asked. We were going along the side of a road crowded with vehicles and troops.

'Fine.'

'I'm tired of this walking.'

'Well, all we have to do is walk now. We don't have to worry.'

'Bonello was a fool.'

'He was a fool all right.'

'What will you do about him, Tenente?'

'I don't know.'

'Can't you just put him down as taken prisoner?'

'I don't know.'

'You see if the war went on they would make bad trouble for his family.'

'The war won't go on,' a soldier said. 'We're going home. The war is over.'

'Everybody's going home.'

'We're all going home.'

'Come on, Tenente,' Piani said. He wanted to get past them.

'Tenente? Who's a Tenente? *A basso gli ufficiali!* Down with officers!'

Piani took me by the arm. 'I better call you by your name,' he said. 'They might try and make trouble. They've shot some officers.' We worked up past them.

'I won't make a report that will make trouble for his family.' I went on with our conversation.

'If the war is over it makes no difference,' Piani said. 'But I don't believe it's over. It's too good that it should be over.'

'We'll know pretty soon,' I said.

'I don't believe it's over. They all think it's over but I don't believe it.'

'*Viva la Pace!*' a soldier shouted. 'We're going home!'

'It would be fine if we all went home,' Piani said. 'Wouldn't you like to go home?'

'Yes.'

'We'll never go. I don't think it's over.'

'*Andiamo a casa!*' a soldier shouted.

'They throw away their rifles,' Piani said. 'They take them off and drop them down while they're marching. Then they shout.'

'They ought to keep their rifles.'

'They think if they throw away their rifles they can't make them fight.'

In the dark and rain, making our way along the side of the road I could see that many of the troops still had their rifles. They stuck up above their capes.

'What brigade are you?' an officer called out.

'*Brigata di Pace,*' some one shouted. 'Peace Brigade!' The officer said nothing.

'What does he say? What does the officer say?'

'Down with the officer. *Viva la Pace!*'

'Come on,' Piani said. We passed two British ambulances,

abandoned in the block of vehicles.

'They're from Gorizia,' Piani said. 'I know the cars.'

'They got further than we did.'

'They started earlier.'

'I wonder where the drivers are?'

'Up ahead probably.'

'The Germans have stopped outside Udine,' I said. 'These people will all get across the river.'

'Yes,' Piani said. 'That's why I think the war will go on.'

'The Germans could come on,' I said. 'I wonder why they don't come one.'

'I don't know. I don't know anything about this kind of war.'

'They have to wait for their transport, I suppose.'

'I don't know,' Piani said. Alone he was much gentler. When he was with the others he was a very rough talker.

'Are you married, Luigi?'

'You know I am married.'

'Is that why you did not want to be a prisoner?'

'That is one reason. Are you married, Tenente?'

'No.'

'Neither is Bonello.'

'You can't tell anything by a man's being married. But I think a married man would want to get back to his wife,' I said. I would be glad to talk about wives.

'Yes.'

'How are your feet?'

'They're sore enough.'

Before daylight we reached the bank of the Tagliamento and followed down along the flooded river to the bridge where all the traffic was crossing.

'They ought to be able to hold at this river,' Piani said. In the dark the flood looked high. The water swirled and it was wide. The wooden bridge was nearly three-quarters of a mile across, and the river, that usually ran in narrow channels in the wide stony bed far below the bridge, was close under the wooden planking. We went along the bank and then worked our way into the crowd that were crosssing the bridge. Crossing slowly in the rain a few feet above the flood, pressed tight in the crowd, the box of an artillery caisson just ahead, I looked over the side and watched the river. Now that we could not go our own pace I felt very tired. There was no exhilaration in crossing the bridge. I wondered what it would be like if a plane bombed it in the daytime.

'Piani,' I said.

'Here I am, Tenente.' He was a little ahead in the jam. No one was talking. They were all trying to get across as soon as they could: thinking only of that. We were almost across. At the far end of the bridge there were officers and carabinieri standing on both sides flashing lights. I saw them silhouetted against the sky-line. As we came close to them I saw one of the officers point to a man in the column. A carabiniere went in after him and came out holding the man by the arm. He took him away from the road. We came almost opposite them. The officers were scrutinizing every one in the column, sometimes speaking to each other, going forward to flash a light in some one's face. They took some one else out just before we came opposite. I saw the man. He was a lieutenant-colonel. I saw the stars in the box on his sleeve as they flashed a light on him. His hair was grey and he was short and fat. The carabiniere pulled him in behind the line of officers. As we came opposite I saw one or two of them look at me. Then one pointed at me and spoke to a carabiniere. I saw the carabiniere start for me, come through the edge of the column toward me, then felt him take me by the collar.

'What's the matter with you?' I said and hit him in the face. I saw his face under the hat, upturned mustaches and blood coming down his cheek. Another one dove in towards us.

'What's the matter with you?' I said. He did not answer. He was watching a chance to grab me. I put my arm behind me to loosen my pistol.

'Don't you know you can't touch an officer?'

The other one grabbed me from behind and pulled my arm up so that it twisted in the socket. I turned with him and the other one grabbed me around the neck. I kicked his shins and got my left knee into his groin.

'Shoot him if he resists,' I heard someone say.

'What's the meaning of this?' I tried to shout but my voice was not very loud. They had me at the side of the road now.

'Shoot him if he resists,' an officer said. 'Take him over back.'

'Who are you?'

'You'll find out.'

'Who are you?'

'Battle police,' another officer said.

'Why don't you ask me to step over instead of having one of these airplanes grab me?'

They did not answer. They did not have to answer. They were battle police.

'Take him back there with the others,' the first officer said.

'You see. He speaks Italian with an accent.'

'So do you, you shit,' I said.

'Take him back with the others,' the first officer said. They took me down behind the line of officers below the road toward a group of people in a field by the river bank. As we walked toward them shots were fired. I saw flashes of the rifles and heard the reports. We came up to the group. There were four officers standing together, with a man in front of them with a carabiniere on each side of him. A group of men were standing guarded by carabinieri. Four other carabinieri stood near the questioning officers, leaning on their carbines. They were wide-hatted carabinieri. The two who had me shoved me with the group waiting to be questioned. I looked at the man the officers were questioning. He was the fat gray-haired little lieutenant-colonel they had taken out of the column. The questioners had all the efficiency, coldness and command of themselves of Italians who are firing and not being fired on.

'Your brigade?'

He told them.

'Regiment?'

He told them.

'Why are you not with your regiment?'

He told them.

'Do you know that an officer should be with his troops?'

He did.

That was all. Another officer spoke.

'It is you and such as you that have let the barbarians onto the sacred soil of the fatherland.'

'I beg your pardon,' said the lieutenant-colonel.

'It is because of treachery such as yours that we have lost the fruits of victory.'

'Have you ever been in a retreat?' the lieutenant-colonel asked.

'Italy should never retreat.'

We stood in the rain and listened to this. We were facing the officers and the prisoner stood in front and a little to one side of us.

'If you are going to shoot me,' the lieutenant-colonel said, 'please shoot me at once without further questioning. The questioning is stupid.' He made the sign of the cross. The officers spoke together. One wrote something on a pad of paper.

'Abandoned his troops, ordered to be shot,' he said.

Two carabinieri took the lieutenant-colonel to the river bank. He walked in the rain, an old man with his hat off, a carabiniere on either side. I did not watch them shoot him but I heard the shots. They were questioning some one else. This officer too was separated from his troops. He was not allowed to make an explanation. He cried when they read the sentence from the pad of paper, and they were questioning another when they shot him. They made a point of being intent on questioning the next man while the man who had been questioned before was being shot. In this way there was obviously nothing they could do about it. I did not know whether I should wait to be questioned or make a break now. I was obviously a German in Italian uniform. I saw how their minds worked; if they had minds and if they worked. They were all young men and they were saving their country. The second army was being re-formed beyond the Tagliamento. They were executing officers of the rank of major and above who were separated from their troops. They were also dealing summarily with German agitators in Italian uniform. They wore steel helmets. Only two of us had steel helmets. Some of the carabinieri had them. The other carabinieri wore the wide hat. Airplanes we called them. We stood in the rain and were taken out one at a time to be questioned and shot. So far they had shot every one that they had questioned. The questioners had that beautiful detachment and devotion to stern justice of men dealing in death without being in any danger of it. They were questioning a full colonel of a line regiment. Three more officers had just been put in with us.

'Where was his regiment?'

I looked at the carabinieri. They were looking at the newcomers. The others were looking at the colonel. I ducked down, pushed between two men, and ran for the river, my head down. I tripped at the edge and went in with a splash. The water was very cold and I stayed under as long as I could. I could feel the current swirl me and I stayed under until I thought I could never come up. The minute I came up I took a breath and went down again. It was easy to stay under with so much clothing and my boots. When I came up the second time I saw a piece of timber ahead of me and reached it and held on with one hand. I kept my head behind it and did not even look over it. I did not want to see the bank. There were shots when I ran and shots when I came up the first time. I heard them when I was almost above water. There were no shots now. The piece of timber swung in the current and I held it with one hand. I looked at the bank. It seemed to be going by very fast. Therre was much wood in the stream. The water was very cold. We passed the brush of an island above the water. I held onto the timber with both hands and let it take me along. The shore was out of sight now.

ERNEST HEMINGWAY

Armistice Day, 1918

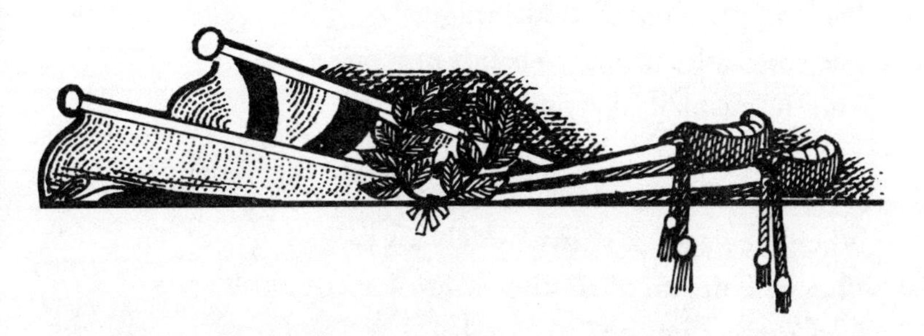

What's all this hubbub and yelling,
Commotion and scamper of feet,
With ear-splitting clatter of kettles and cans,
Wild laughter down Mafeking Street?

O, those are the kids whom we fought for
(You might think they'd been scoffing our rum)
With flags that they waved when we marched off to war
In the rapture of bugle and drum.

Now they'll hang Kaiser Bill from a lamp-post,
Von Tirpitz they'll hang from a tree...
We've been promised a 'Land fit for Heroes' –
What heroes we heroes must be!

And the guns that we took from the Fritzes,
That we paid for with rivers of blood,
Look, they're hauling them down to Old Battersea Bridge
Where they'll topple them, souse, in the mud!

But there's old men and women in corners
With tears falling fast on their cheeks,
There's the armless and legless and sightless –
It's seldom that one of them speaks.

And there's flappers gone drunk and indecent
Their skirts kilted up to the thigh,
The constables lifting no hands in reproof
And the chaplain averting his eye...

When the days of rejoicing are over,
When the flags are stowed safely away,
They will dream of another wild 'War to End Wars'
And another wild Armistice day.

But the boys who were killed in the trenches,
Who fought with no rage and no rant,
We left them stretched out on their pallets of mud
Low down with the worm and the ant.

ROBERT GRAVES

Mayhem In Peacetime

from *'Wingate in Peace and War'*

Orde and I met again in 1932, while he was home on leave, and he told me a good deal about his life in the Sudan. One of the best stories was how he saved the Officers' Mess finances by putting water in the gin. The 'doctored' bottles were not used until the third round of drinks and so the change in strength went unnoticed.

Of the Zerzura expedition, he told me that his equipment consisted of 'a few camels, some cod liver oil, some dates, a compass, and a bathing costume'. When I asked why the latter should have been taken across the desert, he replied that he used it to put over his head during sandstorms. Regarding navigation, he said that he had ridden the leading camel, setting a course with his compass, while at the rear of the column had marched an Arab pushing a bicycle wheel across the sand. Fixed to the wheel was a cyclometer which, theoretically, should have provided an accurate reading of the distance covered. Wingate thought he had hit on a novel way of keeping a check on his position by dead reckoning. But theory was not matched by practice. At the end of the first day's march he found to his dismay that the cyclometer registered a mere 0.4 miles – tiring of pushing the wheel, the Arab had resorted to his natural custom and had carried it on his head.

MAJOR-GENERAL DEREK TULLOCH

The Raincoat

Way back in 1935, when Lord Charteris was a subaltern serving in Burma, he happened to be on duty as the orderly officer.

The monsoon had just started and on reaching the guardroom, he said to the guard commander, 'Sergeant Burridge, before I inspect the guard would you mind hanging my raincoat up inside?'

He then carried out the inspection and eventually returned to the orderly room, realising suddenly that he had left his coat in the guardroom.

He went to the phone and picked it up. 'Sergeant Burridge, orderly officer here. I believe I've left my raincoat there?'

Burridge walked across the floor, held the raincoat up to the earpiece of the 'phone and said, 'Yes, sir – is this one yours?'

T.S. NASH

Trench Digging

In 1938 I was a sapper in the Royal Engineers of the Territorial Army. As a very keen member I used to go to the Duke of York's Headquarters in Chelsea for training, usually some three times a week, in the evenings. Training in military engineering in those days differed very little from the engineering carried out during the 1914–18 War.

The Royal Engineers were responsible, among other things, for setting up trench slits. This was done by placing white tape showing the layout of the system, then digging them out.

One of the most frequently used types was called a bastion trench which was in use throughout the Great War.

One summer evening we marched from the Duke of York's HQ to a nearby school for an exercise in setting out and digging a bastion trench. We used the asphalt playground and were detailed off so that a start could be made on laying down the marking tape. When this was completed each sapper was given a task, that task being to shift a quantity of earth in a given time, the earth from the trench to be piled in front to form the parapet and the rear to form the defence there.

At this juncture we were told that the school playground was temporarily leased to the War Department and under no circumstances was the surface to be damaged in any way. Therefore we had strict instructions to lift the pick-axe to shoulder height, bring it smartly down and, with the greatest of care, stop it an inch or two above the ground.

This continued for some time until we had supposedly loosened an amount of soil. The pick-axe was put on one side. A shovel was then used very carefully to shovel up the non-existent soil, making sure of course that at no point did the shovel touch the playground. Thus we built up the totally imaginary parapet and rear baffle.

This continued for two hours before we finally marched back to the Duke of York's HQ and were dismissed. I remember this incident so vividly because I was severely taken to task for enquiring if we were to go back the following evening to fill in the trenches we had not dug.

P.E. TIDY

A World in Turmoil 1939-45

Basic Defence

In November 1984 Lieutenant General Pringle, former Commandant of the Royal Marines and then Chairman of the Chatham Historic Dockyard Trust, made a startling discovery. He noticed that throughout the yard cannon removed from ships of the line had been put to practical use: what was probably the finest collection of naval ordnance in the world was now serving out its time as bollards and gateposts, unremarked by anyone. Since his brief was to preserve the dockyard as a museum he made it his top priority to have them removed and restored. (This was reported in the Peterborough column of the *Daily Telegraph* in December 1984).

On reading this my mind went back to 1939 when I was stationed at the Royal School of Military Engineering as an instructor, no better informed on matters historic than any of my colleagues. At that time it was decided that some means of airfield defence should be formulated and someone had the idea of using large lorries with the superstructure taken off to leave a flat base, thus rendering them suitable for use as travelling anti-aircraft platforms.

The idea was to build a form of reinforced concrete pill-box on the flat base, probably to house heavy machine-guns which could then engage any low-flying German aircraft coming over the airfield to harass RAF operations. At that time I was a Staff-sergeant Instructor specialising in reinforced concrete engineering and was detailed off to investigate the feasibility of these lorries being used in such a manner.

Obviously the first thing to discover was whether or not the vehicles would be capable of carrying such a load across rough terrain. What I needed therefore was something approximately of the same weight as I calculated the pill-boxes would be and I was having no luck finding anything suitable until I came across the 'bollards' in Chatham dockyard.

In no time I had two of them taken up and mounted on the lorries. Then they were driven about the town for testing. It seemed a good idea to me – after all, I was only conducting an experiment – but the towns-people took a different view of the matter. They were unimpressed that such antique weaponry was being pressed into service apparently for their air defence.

The trials were terminated and the idea abandoned. And two pieces of history were returned to their usual place until Lieutenant General Pringle came on the scene all those years later.

P.E. TIDY

RAMC

In December 1939, I was second-in-command of 'A' Company of the 2 Lincolns, stationed just north-east of Lille at Petit Ronchin. I fell ill with appendicitis.

From the Regimental Aid Post I travelled with all my kit to the Casualty Clearing Station at Cambrai where I was bedded down for two days, then taken by ambulance to the hospital train. There I was allotted a bunk and fed on bully-beef sandwiches. I later learned that the RAMC staff had been selling the special sick rations to the French.

Arriving at the base hospital at Le Treport, I found that it was not ready for patients, lit only by oil lamps and with nothing better than Valor paraffin stoves to fight the bitter cold. After a desperately uncomfortable night, I and others were piled into ambulances and driven to No. 1 General Hospital in the Casino at Dieppe, where at last conditions were excellent and I was given the treatment so badly needed.

But at some time during my travels someone had stolen a gold cross from around my neck. As someone dryly observed to me, during the First World War RAMC was said to stand for Rob All My Comrades.

MAJOR F.D. GOODE

Dakar

The Dakar Expedition of 1940 was a military shambles and there was good reason for it: the enemy was ready and waiting. The Vichy French had learned all they needed by quite simple means:

1) De Gaulle had given a dinner for his officers in London and publicly toasted Dakar;

2) The Ordnance Depot at Donnington consigned all the stores for the expedition in packing cases proudly stencilled DAKAR.

Who needs undercover agents?

MAJOR F.D. GOODE

The RAF Regiment

For me the turning point of the war was reached on July 5th, 1940. I tottered into the RAF recruiting depot at St. Pancras, eight stone of skin and bones loosely wrapped in a length of five feet, eleven inches. I had a physique that resembled a bent bean-pole and a complexion that looked as though I had been covered with two coats of Dulux White. I told the Medical Officer that I wanted to be a pilot. He replied that he wanted to be Governor of Bermuda but couldn't see much hope of either of us fulfilling out ambitions.

Since the outbreak of war I had tried three times to join the Royal Navy and twice the Army. For my troubles I had received five rejections. One examining doctor had told me to go home and stay in bed until the war was over. Another had advised me never to run for buses and to avoid walking up stairs. I was convinced that there was a conspiracy afoot by Nazi agents posing as doctors to prevent me from entering the conflict.

Mind you, I must admit that I was colour blind and had a peculiar affliction that prevented me from closing one eye at a time. It was a matter of both eyes shut or both open. Then too, unfavourable decisions were probably influenced by the fact that I had been bed ridden for seven years with rheumatic fever and a faulty heart-valve which the doctor insisted upon referring to loftily as Mitral Stenosis.

So you will understand that I was not only surprised but literally staggered when the RAF came to the conclusion that 'perhaps I could be of some use'. I almost ran away from the recruiting depot in case someone came after me to explain that it had all been a mistake.

When I told my boss that I had joined the Air Force his incredulous gasp was, 'Not OUR Air Force!'

A colleague thought I would have been more help to Britain if I'd joined the Luftwaffe.

When my mother regained her breath she said that the RAF doctors should be reported to the Medical Council. My father said I would be far more useful if I joined one of the civilian services. But offhand he couldn't think of one which would take me.

Three weeks later I reported for initial training, for which I had prepared myself by jumping out of bed promptly every morning and immediately doing two or three press ups. By some miracle I survived the first week of it with only minor failures, though the abuse and bad language from the NCOs directed at myself grew. The climax of my disasters came, however, when a sergeant instructed us, his new recruits, in target shooting. Six of us were sprawled on the ground, each with a Lee Enfield rifle and five rounds of ammunition. The targets looked as though they were at least ten miles away, but the recruits to each side of me appeared undeterred.

It was unfortunate that the sergeant was unaware of my eye affliction because after we had fired and the targets were checked, the man on my right had scored seven hits with his five bullets and the man on my left six. My target was completely unmarked. At first I thought I had been issued with blanks, but mature reflection convinced me otherwise. For a long time afterward, and when the sergeant had given up his struggle to find new names to call me, I wondered where the other two shots had gone. Back to their maker, like the rest of us, I supposed.

It was rumoured that the NCO instructors were to have a celebratory party when I was posted away. At the very least they must have been greatly relieved to see me on my way to a Bomber Command Squadron in Yorkshire.

After an assortment of tasks that didn't seem to be of much help to the war effort I became a night guard. I had heard that German Junkers 88s had developed the habit of following our aircraft home from raids and then bombing and strafing the aerodromes they headed for, but for several nights I stood my guard and nothing happened. All that was required of me was to be present and armed with my trusty rifle and three rounds of ammunition – about as much use to me as a water-pistol.

But eventually our turn came and one night at 3 a.m. all hell was let loose. Our bombers were coming in and so were the Jerry dive bombers. Camp buildings were hit and incendiaries started fires everywhere while our aircraft did their best to make it to the deck, not all of them succeeding. There was nothing for it but to take cover and watch the devastation, a mere spectator to this gigantic firework display which succeeded in killing the Station Commander and thirteen airmen. Many more were injured.

Such raids now occurred repeatedly and the lack of defence against them appalled me. The Germans raided with impunity, wreaking their havoc and then vanishing into the night.

Men were dying, vital equipment was being wasted and I could see no justification for it, so finally I wrote to Will Hipwell, editor of the Forces newspaper *Reveille,* and asked him to urge that action be taken on airfield defence. Hipwell was a go getter of a journalist who had somehow coaxed the government into allowing him a ration of newsprint to produce his paper for worldwide distribution to all the Armed Forces. He gave my story front page prominence. This was immediately followed up by John Gordon, editor of the *Sunday Express.* In the Commons, MPs pressed the Home Secretary, Herbert Morrison (a pacifist in the First World War) as to whether there was any truth in what was being alleged in the press. An angry Herbert Morrison threatened to withdraw the allocation of newsprint from the *Reveille,* thought it was noticeable that no such threat was made to the *Sunday Express,* possibly because it was owned by Lord Beaverbrook, a man possessing quite enough power to fight back and create widespread unpleasantness.

Shortly afterward, the necessary armaments began to flow through to the RAF and, most importantly, the RAF Regiment was formed. This was a trained army within the service and filled a desperate need. In his War Memoirs, Winston Churchill later wrote that by 1942 the RAF Regiment was a force of 60,000 men.

Forty years after my campaign, in April 1981, I received a

letter from the Ministry of Defence acknowledging my part in the formation of the regiment. It was sent with the compliments of the Officer Commanding the Royal Air Force.

This warmed me greatly because it proved that, though I'd been incapable of achieving anything with a rifle, I had certainly managed to do so with a pen.

TOM E. CHILTON

The Invaders

We retired early to bed and slept until, at two o'clock in the morning, a gillie banged on the door. Colin got up, took from the gillie's hand a telegram, opened it, and read it. It said: SQUADRON MOVING SOUTH STOP CAR WILL FETCH YOU AT EIGHT O'CLOCK DENHOLM. For us, the war began that night.

At ten o'clock we were back at Turnhouse. The rest of the Squadron were all set to leave; we were to move down to Hornchurch, an airdrome twelve miles east of London on the Thames Estuary. Four machines would not be serviceable until the evening and Broody Benson, Pip Cardell, Colin, and I were to fly them down. We took off at four o'clock, some five hours after the others, Broody leading, Pip and I to each side, and Colin in the box, map reading. Twenty-four of us flew south that 10th day of August 1941: of those twenty-four eight were to fly back.

We landed at Hornchurch at about seven o'clock to receive our first shock. Instead of one section there were four Squadrons at readiness; 603 Squadron were already in action.

They started coming in about half an hour after we landed, smoke stains along the leading edges of the wings showing that all the guns had been fired. They had acquitted themselves well although caught at a disadvantage of height.

'You don't have to look for them,' said Brian. 'You have to look for a way out.'

From this flight MacDonald did not return.

At this time the Germans were sending up comparatively few bombers. They were making a determined attempt to wipe out our entire Fighter Force and from dawn till dusk the sky was filled with Messerschmitt 109's and 110's.

Half a dozen of us always slept at the Dispersal Hut to be ready for a surprise enemy attack at dawn. This entailed being up by four-thirty, and by five o'clock having our machines warmed up and the oxygen, sights, and ammunition tested. The first Hun attack usually came over about breakfast time and from then until eight o'clock at night we were almost continuously in the air. We ate when we could, baked beans and bacon and eggs being sent over from the Mess.

On the morning after our arrival I walked over with Peter Howes and Broody. Howes was at Hornchurch with another Squadron and worried because he had as yet shot nothing down. Every evening when we came into the Mess he would ask us how many we had got and then go over miserably to his room. His Squadron had had a number of losses and was due for relief. If ever a man needed it, it was Howes. Broody, on the other hand, was in a high state of excitement, his sharp eager face grinning from ear to ear. We left Howes at his Dispersal Hut and walked over to where our machines were being warmed up. The voice of the controller came unhurried over the loud speaker, telling us to take off, and in a few seconds we were running for our machines. I climbed into the cockpit of my plane and felt an empty sensation of suspense in the pit of my stomach. For one second time seemed to stand still and I stared blankly in front of me. I knew that morning I was to kill for the first time. That I might be killed or in any way injured did not occur to me. Later, when we were losing pilots regularly, I did consider it in an abstract way when on the ground; but once in the air, never. I knew it could not happen to me. I suppose every pilot knows that, knows it cannot happen to him; even when he is taking off for the last time, when he will not return, he knows that he cannot be killed. I wondered idly what he was like, this man I would kill. Was he young, was he fat, would he die with the Fuhrer's name on his lips, or would he die alone, in that last moment conscious of himself as a man? I would never know. Then I was being strapped in, my mind automatically checking the controls, and we were off.

We ran into them at 18,000 feet, twenty yellow-nosed Messerschmitt 109's, above five hundred feet above us. Our Squadron strength was eight, and as they came down on us we went into line astern and turned head on to them. Brian Carberry, who was leading the Section dropped the nose of his machine, and I could almost feel the leading Nazi pilot push forward on his stick to bring his guns to bear. At the same moment Brian hauled hard back on his own control stick and led us over them in a steep climbing turn to the left. In two vital seconds they lost their advantage. I saw Brian let go a burst of fire at the leading plane, saw the pilot put his machine into a half roll, and knew that he was mine. Automatically, I kicked the rudder to the left to get him at right angles, turned the gun button to 'Fire,' and let go a four-second burst with full deflection. He came right through my sights and I saw the tracer from all eight guns thud home. For a second he seemed to hang motionless; then a jet of red flame shot upwards and he spun to the ground.

For the next few minutes I was too busy looking after myself to think of anything, but when, after a short while, they turned and made off over the Channel, and we were ordered to our base, my mind began to work again.

It had happened.

My first emotion was one of satisfaction, satisfaction at a job adequately done, at the final logical conclusion of months of specialized training. And then I had a feeling of the essential rightness of it all. He was dead and I was alive; it could so easily have been the other way round; and that would somehow have been right too. I realized in that moment just how lucky a fighter pilot is. He has none of the personalized emotions of the soldier, handed a rifle and bayonet and told to charge. He does not even have to share the dangerous emotions of the bomber pilot who night after night must experience that childhood longing for smashing things. The fighter pilot's emotions are those of the duelist – cool, precise, impersonal. He is privileged to kill well. For if one must either kill or be killed, as now one must, it should, I feel, be done with dignity. Death should be given the setting it deserves; it should never be a pettiness; and for the fighter pilot it never can be.

From this flight Broody Benson did not return.

During that August-September period we were always so outnumbered that it was practically impossible, unless we were lucky enough to have the advantage of height, to deliver more than one Squadron attack. After a few seconds we always broke up, and the sky was a smoke trail of individual dog-fights. The result was that the Squadron would come home individually, machines landing one after the other at intervals of about two minutes. After an hour, Uncle George would make a check-up on who was missing. Often there would be a telephone call from some pilot to say that he had made a forced landing at some other airdrome, or in a field. But the telephone wasn't always so welcome. It would be a rescue squad announcing the number of a crashed machine; then Uncle George would check it, and cross another name off the list. At that time, the losing of pilots was somehow extremely impersonal; nobody, I think, felt any great emotion – there simply wasn't time for it.

After the hard lesson of the first two days, we became more canny and determined not to let ourselves be caught from above. We would fly on the reciprocal of the course given us by the controller until we got to 15,000 feet, and then fly back again, climbing all the time. By this means we usually saw the Huns coming in below us, and were in a perfect position to deliver a Squadron attack. If caught at a disadvantage, they would never stay to fight, but always turned straight back for the Channel. We arranged a system whereby two planes always flew together – thus if one should follow a plane down the other stayed 500 feet or so above, to protect him from attack in the rear.

Often, machines would come back to their base just long enough for the ground staff, who worked with beautiful speed, to refuel them and put in a new oxygen bottle and more ammunition before taking off again. Uncle George was shot down several times but always turned up unhurt; once we thought Rusty was gone for good, but he was back leading his flight the next day; one sergeant pilot in 'A' Flight was shot down four times, but he seemed to bear a charmed life.

The sun and the great height at which we flew often made it extremely difficult to pick out the enemy machines, but it was here that Shep's experience on the moors of Scotland proved invaluable. He led the guard section and always saw the Huns long before anyone else. For me the sun presented a major problem. We had dark lenses on our glasses, but I never wore mine. They gave me a feeling of claustrophobia. With spots on the windscreen, spots before the eyes, and a couple of spots which might be Messerschmitts, blind spots on my goggles seemed too much of a good thing; I always slipped them up on my forehead before going into action. For this and for not wearing gloves I paid a stiff price.

I remember once going practically to France before shooting down a 109. There were two of them, flying at sea-level and headed for the French Coast. Raspberry was flying beside me and caught one halfway across. I got right up close behind the second one and gave it a series of short bursts. It darted about in front, like a startled rabbit, and finally plunged into the sea about three miles off the French Coast.

On another occasion, I was stupid enough to actually fly over France: the sky appeared to be perfectly clear but for one returning Messerschmitt, flying very high. I had been trying to catch him for about ten minutes and was determined that he should not get away.

Eventually I caught him inland from Calais and was just about to open fire when I saw a squadron of twelve Messerschmitts coming in on my right. I was extremely frightened, but turned in towards them and opened fire at the leader. I could see his tracer going past underneath me, and then saw his hood fly off, and the next moment they were past. I didn't wait to see anymore, but made off for home, pursued for half the distance by eleven very determined Germans. I landed a good hour after everyone else to find Uncle George just finishing his check up.

From this flight Larry Cunningham did not return.

After about a week at Hornchurch, I woke late one morning to the noise of machines running up on the airdrome. It irritated me: I had a headache.

Having been on every flight the previous day, the morning was mine to do with as I pleased. I got up slowly, gazed dispassionately at my tongue in the mirror, and wandered over to the Mess for breakfast. It must have been getting on for twelve o'clock when I came out on to the airdrome to find the usual August heat haze forming a dull pall over everything. I started to walk across the airdrome to the Dispersal Point on the far side. There were only two machines on the ground so I concluded that the squadron was already up. Then I heard a shout, and our ground crew drew up in a lorry beside me. Sergeant Ross leaned out:

'Want a lift, sir? We're going round.'

'No thanks, Sergeant. I'm going to cut across.'

This was forbidden for obvious reasons, but I felt like that.

'OK, sir. See you round there.'

The lorry trundled off down the road in a cloud of dust. I walked on across the landing ground. At that moment I heard the voice of the controller.

'Large enemy bombing formation approaching Hornchurch. All personnel not engaged in active duty take cover immediately.'

I looked up. They were still not visible. At the Dispersal Point I saw Bubble and Pip Cardell make a dash for the shelter. Three Spitfires just landed, turned about and came past me with a roar to take off down wind. Our lorry was still trundling along the road, maybe half way round, and seemed suddenly an awful long way from the Dispersal Point.

I looked up again, and this time I saw them – about a dozen slugs, shining in the bright sun and coming straight on. At the rising scream of the first bomb I instinctively shrugged up my shoulders and ducked my head. Out of the corner of my eye I saw the three Spitfires. One moment they were about twenty feet up in close formation; the next, catapulted apart as though on elastic. The leader went over on his back and ploughed along the runway with a rending crash of tearing fabric; number 2 put a wing in and spun round on his airscrew, while the plane on the left was blasted wingless into the next field. I remember thinking stupidly, 'That's the shortest flight he's ever taken,' and then my feet were nearly knocked from under me, my mouth was full of dirt, and Bubble, gesticulating like a madman from the shelter entrance was yelling: 'Run, you bloody fool, run!' I ran. Suddenly awakened to the lunacy of my behaviour, I covered the distance to that shelter as if impelled by a rocket and shot through the entrance while once again the ground rose up and hit me, and my head smashed hard against one of the pillars. I subsided on a heap of rubble and massaged it.

'Who's here?' I asked, peering through the gloom.

'Cardell and I and three of our ground crew,' said Bubble, 'and, by the Grace of God, you!'

I could see by his mouth that he was still talking but a sudden concentration of the scream and crump of falling bombs made it impossible to hear him.

The air was thick with dust and the shelter shook and heaved at each explosion, yet somehow held firm. For about three minutes the bedlam continued, and then suddenly ceased. In the utter silence which followed, nobody moved. None of us wished to be the first to look on the devastation which we felt must be outside. Then Bubble spoke. 'Praise God!' he said. 'I'm not a civilian. Of all the bloody frightening things I've ever done, sitting in that shelter was the worst. Me for the air from now on!'

It broke the tension and we scrambled out of the entrance. The runways were certainly in something of a mess. Gaping holes and great gobbets of earth were everywhere. Right in front of us a bomb had landed by my Spitfire, covering it with a shower of grit and rubble.

I turned to the aircraftsman standing beside me. 'Will you get hold of Sergeant Ross and tell him to have a crew give her an inspection.'

He jerked his head toward one corner of the airdrome: 'I think I'd better collect the crew myself, sir. Sergeant Ross won't be doing any more inspections.'

I followed his glance and saw the lorry, the roof about twenty yards away, lying grotesquely on its side. I climbed into the cockpit, and, feeling faintly sick, tested out the switches. Bubble poked his head over the side.

'Let's go over to the Mess and see what's up: all our machines will be landing down at the reserve landing field anyway.'

I climbed out and walked over to find the three Spitfire pilots celebrating in the bar, quite unharmed but for a few superficial scratches, in spite of being machine-gunned by the bombers. 'Operations' was undamaged: no hangar had been touched and the Officers' Mess had two windows broken.

The station commander ordered every available man and woman on to the job of repairing the airdrome surface and by four o'clock there was not a hole to be seen. Several unexploded bombs were marked off, and two lines of yellow flags were laid down to mark the runways. At five o'clock our squadron, taking off for a 'flap' from the reserve field, landed safely on its home base. Thus, apart from four men killed in the lorry and a network of holes on the landing surface, there was nothing to show for ten minutes' really accurate bombing from 12,000 feet, in which several dozen sticks of bombs had been dropped. It was striking proof of the inefficacy of their attempts to wipe out our advance fighter airdromes.

Brian had a bullet through his foot, and as my machine was still out of commission, I took his place in readiness for the next show. I had had enough of the ground for one day.

Six o'clock came and went, and no call. We started to play poker and I was winning. It was agreed that we should stop at seven: should there be a 'flap' before then, the game was off. I gazed anxiously at the clock. I am always unlucky at cards, but when the hands pointed to 6:55 I really began to feel my luck was on the change. But sure enough at that moment came the voice of the controller: '603 Squadron take off and patrol base: further instructions in the air.'

We made a dash for our machines and within two minutes were off the ground. Twice we circled the airdrome to allow all twelve planes to get in formation. We were flying in four sections of three: red section leading, blue and green to right and left, and the three remaining planes forming a guard section above and behind us.

I was flying No. 2 in the blue section.

Over the radio came the voice of the controller: 'Hullo Red Leader.' And then the instructions and their acknowledgement by the leader.

As always, for the first few minutes we flew on the reciprocal of the course given until we reached 15,000 feet. We then turned about and flew on 110 degrees in an all-out climb, thus coming out of the sun and gaining height all the way.

During the climb Uncle George was in constant touch with the ground. We were to intercept about 20 enemy fighters at 25,000 feet. I glanced across at Stapme and saw his mouth moving. That meant he was singing again. He would sometimes do this with the radio on 'send,' with the result that mingled with our instructions from the ground we would hear a raucous rendering of 'Night and Day.' And then quite clearly over the radio I heard the German excitedly calling to each other. This was a not infrequent occurrence and it made one feel that they were right behind, although often they were some distance away. I switched my set to 'send' and called out *'Halts Maul!'* and as many other choice pieces of German invective as I could remember. To my delight I heard one of them answer: 'You feelthy Englishmen, we will teach you how to speak to a German.' I am aware that this sounds a tall story, but several others in the Squadron were listening out and heard the whole thing.

I looked down. It was a completely cloudless sky and way below lay the English countryside, stretching lazily into the distance, a quite extraordinary picture of green and purple in the setting sun.

I took a glance at my altimeter. We were at 28,000 feet. At that moment Shep yelled 'Tallyho' and dropped down in front of Uncle George in a slow dive in the direction of the approaching planes. Uncle George saw them at once.

'OK. Lie astern.'

I drew in behind Stapme and took a look at them. They were about 2,000 feet below us, which was a pleasant change, but they must have spotted us at the same moment, for they were forming a protective circle, one behind the other, which is a defence formation hard to break.

'Echelon starboard,' came Uncle George's voice.

We spread out fanwise to the right.

'Going down!'

One after the other we peeled off in a power dive. I picked out one machine and switched my gun button to 'Fire.' At 300 yards I had him in my sights. At 200 I opened up in a long four-second burst and saw the tracer going into his nose. Then I was pulling out, so hard that I could feel my eyes dropping through my neck. Coming round in a slow climbing turn I saw that we had broken them up. The sky was now a mass of individual dog-fights. Several of them had already been knocked down. One, I hoped was mine, but on pulling up I had not been able to see the result. To my left I saw Peter Pease make a head-on attack on a Messerschmitt. They were headed straight for each other and it looked as though the fire of both was striking home. Then at the last minute the Messerschmitt pulled up taking Peter's fire full in the belly. It rolled onto its back, yellow flames pouring from the cockpit, and vanished.

The next few minutes were typical. First the sky a bedlam of machines; then suddenly silence and not a plane to be seen. I noticed then that I was very tired and very hot. The sweat was running down my face in rivulets. But this was no time for vague reflections. Flying around the sky on one's own at that time was not a healthy course of action.

I still had some ammunition left. Having no desire to return to the airdrome until it had all been used to some good purpose, I took a look around the sky for some friendly fighters. About a mile away over Dungeness I saw a formation of about forty Hurricanes on patrol at 20,000 feet. Feeling that there was safety in numbers, I set off in their direction. When about 200 yards from the rear machine, I looked down and saw 5,000 feet below another formation of fifty machines flying in the same direction. Flying stepped up like this was an old trick of the Huns, and I was glad to see we were adopting the same tactics. But as though hit by a douche of cold water, I suddenly woke up. There were far more machines flying together than we could ever muster over one spot. I took another look at the rear machine in my formation, and sure enough, there was the Swastika on its tail. Yet they all seemed quite oblivious of my presence. I had the sun behind me and a glorious opportunity. Closing in to 150 yards I let go a three-second burst into the rear machine. It flicked onto its back and spun out of sight. Feeling like an irresponsible schoolboy who has perpetrated some crime which must inevitably be found out, I glanced round me. Still nobody seemed disturbed. I suppose I could have repeated the performance on the next machine, but I felt that it was inadvisable to tempt Providence too far. I did a quick half roll and made off home, where I found to my irritation that Raspberry, as usual had three planes down to my one.

There was to be a concert on the Station that night, but as I had to be up at five the next morning for Dawn Patrol, I had a quick dinner and two beers, and went to bed, feeling not unsatisfied with the day.

Perhaps the most amusing though painful experience which I had was when I was shot down acting as arse-end Charlie to a Squadron of Hurricanes. Arse-end Charlie is the man who weaves backwards and forwards above and behind the Squadron to protect them from attack from the rear. There had been the usual dog-fights over the South Coast, and the Squadron had broken up. Having fired one snap burst, I climbed up in search of friendly Spitfires, but found instead a squadron of Hurricanes flying round the sky at 18,000 feet in sections of stepped-up threes, but with no rear guard. So I joined on. I learned within a few seconds the truth of the old warning, 'Beware of the Hun in the Sun.' I was making pleasant little sweeps from side to side, and peering earnestly in my mirror when, from out of the sun and dead astern, bullets started appearing along my port wing. There is an appalling tendency to sit and watch this happen without taking any action, as though mesmerized by a snake; but I managed to pull myself together and go into spin, at the same time attempting to call up the Hurricanes and warn them, but I found that my radio had been shot away. At first there appeared to be little damage done and I started to climb up again, but black smoke began pouring out of the engine and there was an unpleasant smell of escaping glycol. I thought I had better get home while I could; but as the windscreen was covered with oil I realized that I couldn't make it and decided instead to put down at Lympne, where there was an airdrome. Then I realized that I wasn't going to make Lympne either – I was going at full boost and only clocking 90 miles per hour, so I decided that I had better put down in the nearest field before I stalled and spun in. I chose a cornfield and put the machine down on its belly. Fortunately nothing caught fire, and I had just climbed out and switched off the petrol, when to my amazement I saw an ambulance coming through the gate. This I thought was real service, until the corporal and two orderlies who climbed out started cantering away in the opposite direction, their necks craned up to the heavens. I looked up and saw about 50 yards away a parachute, and suspended on the air, his legs dangling vaguely, Colin. He was a little burned about his face and hands but quite cheerful.

We were at once surrounded by a bevy of officers and discovered that we had landed practically in the back garden of a Brigade cocktail party. A salvage crew from Lympne took charge of my machine, a doctor took charge of Colin, and the rest took charge of me, handing me double whiskies for the nerves at a laudable rate. I was put up that night by the Brigadier, who thought I was suffering from rather severe shock, largely because by dinner time I was so pie-eyed that I didn't dare open my mouth but answered all his questions with a glassy stare. The next day I went up to London by train, a somewhat incongruous figure, carrying a helmet and parachute. The prospect of a long and tedious journey by tube to Hornchurch did not appeal to me, so I called up the Air Ministry and demanded a car and a WAAF. I was put on to the good lady in charge of transport, a sergeant, who protested apologetically that she must have the authorization of a Wing Commander. I told her forcibly that at this moment I was considerably more important than any Wing Commander, painted a vivid picture of the complete disorganization of Fighter Command in the event of my not being back at Hornchurch within an hour, and clinched the argument by telling her that my parachute was a military secret which must on no account be seen in a train. By the afternoon I was flying again.

That evening there was a terrific attack on Hornchurch and for the first time since coming south, I saw some bombers. There were twelve Dornier 215's flying in close formation at about 12,000 feet, and headed back for France. I was on my way back to the airdrome when I first sighted them about 5,000 feet below me. I dived straight down in a quarter head-on attack. It seemed quite impossible to miss, and I pressed the button. Nothing happened, I had already fired all my ammunition. I could not turn back, so I put both my arms over my head and went straight through the formation, never thinking I'd get out of it unscratched. I landed on the airdrome with the machine riddled with bullets, but quite serviceable.

From this flight Bubble Waterson did not return.

RICHARD HILLARY

The Guard

In 1941 I was an infantryman with the 7th Battalion of the Black Watch, a crack regiment if ever there was one. But I sustained an arm injury and, after several weeks in hospital, was sent to convalesce at Dunblane Hydro, Perthshire, a building perched atop a steeply rising hill.

Here I discovered that towards the end of their convalescence the more able personnel were detailed for Guard Duty. Previous experience – or even the lack of it – was of no account: procedures had to be abided by and rules obeyed. Thus I found myself in some most unusual company.

The Orderly Officer was a Polish Air Force Officer with a very limited English vocabulary, the Orderly Sergeant an Air Force Sergeant, the Guard Commander an Army Catering Corps Corporal, and the Guard itself comprised a motley bunch of airmen, infantrymen and whoever else could be mustered.

The achievements of what can only be described as a rabble had to be seen to be believed, though a peak was reached one day when the Orderly Officer decided to have an inspection parade. While he was dismounting from his horse the Guard was marching past.

'Eyes right!' shouted the Guard Commander, doing the same himself, and correctly saluting at the same time. But out of the corner of his eye he noticed in panic that his men were about to march over the edge of the steep bank.

'Right wheel!' he bawled and this they did, though it was no easy manoeuvre since the corporal had not had sufficient time to give the 'eyes front' order. They trod on each others' heels, collided with each other and generally ended up blundering in all directions. While this was going on, for reasons best known to himself, the corporal was saluting by raising his right arm to his cap while his rifle was still at the slope – for the benefit of the layman, something which is never done. When bearing a rifle the hand is banged on that, when not it goes to the cap, but never, never, never at the same time. The corporal's lame cock-up could not be tolerated. What the devil was this man about?

The Polish Orderly Officer intended to find out. When some sort of order had been restored and the men dismissed he stormed into the Guardroom and confronted the Guard Commander. 'Corporal!' he cried. 'Ze guard. Ze guard is not good.'

'No, sir. Not the best is it?'

'Practice. Zey practice yesterday?'

'Practice what, sir?'

'Ze march-past! Ze guard duty!'

'Difficult, sir.'

'Difficult? Why is zat difficult?'

The Army Catering Corps Corporal had no need to cook up an answer to this one. 'I'd like to help you, sir, but I can't train them in something I've never done in my life before.'

THOMAS ROBERTSON

All Clear

I was NCO i/c PAD Malta 42–43 (the military ARP). We had one air raid, all the HQ staff, OC, CSM, clerks etc, were in the shelter awaiting the 'all clear'. On the signal the HQ corporal opened the thick door to resume work. Just outside, however, was a great big UXB. A 'dud bomb' 4 – 5′ or so in size was standing upright, nose down, just outside the door – TICKING! A horrified shout went up and the company very rapidly dispersed via the other end of the tunnel.

'Very rapidly,' the OC remarked afterwards to the Sgt-Major. 'The fastest I've ever seen the Company move, SARNT MAJOR!'

R.J. SHEARS

Joining Up

My mother, Lily Rose Cook, to do an old friend (crippled and unable to do housework) a favour, would visit her every Thursday and help out for three hours. She would return by dinner time, 1pm, when my father and I would also be home. But this particular week for some reason the day had been changed to Wednesday. So my mother was in someone else's house and my father at work in a big chemical factory – less than a quarter of a mile from each other.

It was the chemical plant the German bombers were after and they hit it while my father was inside. The factory was next to some allotments, separated from them by a high wall.

As the string of bombs dropped the first one fell on the house next to the one where my mother was. That house was completely destroyed and along with it half the house adjoining. My mother was killed instantly. She was 42. The second bomb fell in the allotments within feet of my father, but the separating wall withstood the blast and he was uninjured except for shock.

I arrived home first for dinner just after 1 pm, as did father, and the first obvious question was, 'Where's Mother?'

We waited a few minutes, then my father said, 'You lay the table and I'll go and see if Mum's on the way.'

He returned about half an hour later. At first he was evasive, telling me that Mum was seriously injured and in hospital, but I could tell by the expression on his face that he was not telling the truth and finally forced him to admit that she had been killed. As he slumped into a chair he added, almost as an afterthought, that he had no wish to live any longer.

He had his wish fulfilled a few months later when he died on 14th June 1941 of shock and a broken heart.

From the moment my mother was killed my sole aim was to avenge her death and I vowed I would join the services. So on May 3rd 1942 I went to the recruiting office at Romford, Essex. My 17th birthday had fallen on the day before and I knew you had to be 18 to join the Royal Marines.

'Birth Certificate,' the sergeant said, holding out his hand.

'Sorry, sergeant,' I replied. 'Lost in the bombing.'

He looked at me consideringly for a moment, then nodded and I was in. I still have my service documents and they show my date of birth as 1924 instead of 1925.

JOHN COOK

Jungle Horticulture

In 1942 I found myself in Burma where I was the adjutant of a Royal Engineering unit. Our task was the building of the Tiddim Road through Burma, south to north, the intention being to use it for the movement of men and supplies when we should eventually be prepared to attempt to recapture the whole country.

The terrain was hopeless for such a project and consequently progress was extremely slow. Our task was made no easier by the information that in all probability our communications with Base Headquarters were to be severed, leaving us to operate as a detatched unit, continuing with the construction as best we could. Naturally enough, our immediate concern was with such minor details as eating enough to keep us going through each day, but we need not have worried because some genius at Headquarters India had a stroke of inspiration and the problem was solved – at least on paper.

He had obviously started from the probability that it would be impossible to get supplies to us and had gone in one leap from the problem to the solution. It was this: since we were to be detached we had therefore to be self-sufficient. So we did our best to moderate our surprise when we received a load of packets of seeds – carrots, onions, lettuces, radishes and what-have-you – with the instructions that we were to clear an area in the jungle, plant the seeds and produce a crop sufficient to ensure that we would not have to go without food altogether.

For no good reason and against my better judgement I did in fact arrange for an area to be cleared and the seeds carefully sown; there were those among us who had knowledge of such things. But, our work being what it was, we weren't there long enough to see what the result of our efforts might turn out to be. On we went and our horticultural venture stayed where it was.

It's nice to think though that one day someone straying through the jungles of North Burma will be totally mystified to stumble across a little corner of England, in the form of gigantic wild carrots, onions, lettuces and probably man-eating radishes.

P.E. TIDY

Float, Damn You, Float

Our constant concern in Burma was not so much the work, nor even the jungle conditions, but that of food. No matter how much I protested to HQ the supplies were appalling. Even that which would normally have been acceptable was rendered inedible by the time it reached us and we were living almost entirely on bully-beef and the local biscuits. Such things as dehydrated potatoes, dehydrated onions, tea, sugar and sultanas were either pilfered while en route or, when they finally reached us, were all mixed up together.

The men were growing angry and frustrated so, as adjutant, I finally went in person to deliver my protest. The usual excuses were poured upon me: the difficulties of getting any supplies at all in the first place, the unreliability of the local labour force, transport problems; I had heard it all before and told them so. In fact, I must have been rather insistent that time because they presented me with half a dozen live ducks which I carried back in triumph to the unit.

Their arrival was greeted with considerable warmth, but it was agreed that they were pitiably thin and would not provide a decent meal for all of us. Since they were alive (essential because anything killed had to be consumed quickly or it went rotten) the thing to do was keep them that way and fatten them up until they were ready for the table. Food was no problem because the biscuits we had grown to hate were ideal feed for them. That solved, the next question was how to keep them happy and comfortable, but this too carried a simple answer. Just outside our camp area slit trenches had been dug and, since this was the monsoon season, every one of them was full to the brim with water. We therefore had more ponds than we could ever need for the ducks to swim on.

The plan was to tie a piece of string around a leg of each of the birds, fasten the other end to a stake so that they would not wander, then launch them into one of the slit trenches where they would grow contented and, more to the point, fat. We readily set about our task and finally reached the big moment: the launching ceremony. Six of the men held the ducks above the water, and at a given signal they were lovingly launched into their natural environment.

The cheering died when to our utter bafflement they all sank gently to the bottom of the trench and gave every sign of drowning. We were well aware that most of the animals in

Burma were odd in one way or another, but ducks that sank like stones were a complete novelty. As fast as we could we reeled them in and managed to resuscitate them. But what were we to do with non-floating ducks? And why were they non-floating anyway? They looked normal enough so perhaps they were some new form of sub-species.

This was a mystery that had to be cleared up so back I went to the depot, where my enquiries finally revealed that the ducks had been transported there in a 3-ton truck which also happened to be carrying a load of petrol in 4-gallon tin containers. Now these particular containers were notorious for the way they leaked and what had happened was that a lot of the petrol had ended up on the ducks and dissolved the natural oils which enabled them to float, and in effect remain waterproof. So all they could do was sink.

Swearing never to use one of those 4-gallon containers again, I returned to our camp and we set about making different arrangements. A shallow hole was dug and filled with water and the ducks placed in it. There they were fed and fattened and led a happy life – paddling.

P.E. TIDY

Bribery and Corruption

As an RAF Bomber pilot I spent many nights flying over Germany convinced that it was always the other chap who got shot down, but in May 1942 on the first '1000-bomber' raid, I was the only one of 30 training Wellington pilots from Finningley who failed to return.

After capture I finally ended up at Stalag Luft 3 POW camp at Sagan in eastern Germany, a camp which eventually became famous for 'The Great Escape' and 'the Wooden Horse' films.

Escaping was the main subject of conversation of the officers in this camp, but many attempts failed due to lack of preparation.

When the new north compound was opened an escape organisation was formed to control activities such as tunnelling, security, tailoring of clothes, forgery of passes, maps etc. This involved several hundreds of POWs and was conducted with complete secrecy.

To stand any chance of getting home, a POW had to be suitably dressed and provided with maps, money and passes in case he was challenged by the German police.

German speaking POWs kept in close touch with all the Germans entering the compound, and it was discovered that the cook house corporal was a married man who also had a mistress and was finding life difficult on a corporal's pay. The escape committee promised him an additional wage each week on the understanding that he would provide us with information of train times, troop movements etc, lend us passes for copying by our forgery department and obtain spare parts for our secret camp radio when required.

In this way many escape attempts were facilitated with ease.

GEOFFREY HUGHES

A Troopship in the Tropics

Five thousand souls are here and all are bounded
Too easily perhaps by the ostensible purpose,
Steady as the ploughshare cleaving England,
Of this great ship, obedient to its compass.

The sundeck for the children and the officers
Under the awning, watching the midsea blue
Until the nurses pass with a soft excitement
Rustling the talk of passengers and crew

Deep in the foetid holds of the tiered bunks
Hold restless men who sweat and toss and sob;
The gamblers on the hatches, in the corner
The accordionist and barber do their job.

The smell of oranges and excrement
Moves among those who write uneasy letters
Or slouch about and curse the stray dejection
That chafes them with its hard nostalgic fetters.

But everywhere in this sweltering Utopia,
In the bareheaded crowd's two minutes' silence,
In corners where the shadows lie like water,
Are tranquil pools of crystal-clear reflexion.

Time is no mystery now; this torrid blueness
Blazed in a fortnight from the English winter.
Distance is subject to our moods and wishes.
Only the void of feeling must be filled.

And as the ship makes peace within herself
The simple donors of goodness with rugged features
Move in the crowd and share their crusts of wisdom;
Life does not name her rough undoctored teachers.

Welsh songs surge softly in the circling darkness;
Thoughts sail back like swans to the English winter;
Strange desires drift into the mind;
Time hardens. But the ruthless Now grows kind.

ALUN LEWIS

To a Comrade in Arms

Red fool, my laughing comrade,
Hiding your woman's love
And your man's madness,
Patrolling farther than nowhere
To gain what is nearer than here,
Your face will grow grey as Christ's garments
With the dust of ditches and trenches,
So endlessly faring.

Red fool, my laughing comrade,
Hiding your mystic symbols
Of bread broken for eating
And palm-leaves strewn for welcome,
What foe will you make your peace with
This summer that is more cruel
Than the ancient God of the Hebrews?

When bees swarm in your nostrils
And honey drips from the sockets
Of eyes that today are frantic
With love that is frustrate,
What vow shall we vow who love you
For the self that you did not value?

ALUN LEWIS

from *'ffundamental ffolkes'*

I was called up in 1943 at the statutory age of 18 and having a deep hatred of the Nazis from school days, made no objection. We were well on the way to winning the war by then and mine was what is lightly called 'a good war': ie: I survived and went round the world. Literally – out through the Panama Canal and back through Suez. During my three years of service, I drew incessantly – but never the exotic and often exciting world around me. It was always fantasies – outlines for drawings or paintings that would be completed when I got back home. Once actually back, I tore up nearly everything. One exception was 'The Immaculate Dead', completed in Chelsea at the tender age of 21 and signed with my true initials. It may be pretentious, but serves as a homage to that impossible master to follow – William Blake.

It was on an island called Manus bang on the Equator, which the Royal Navy and the Americans were occupying at the time, that I first began my preoccupation with ffauna. I was occupying the outdoor and very primitive casey for four (mostly attended) when something fell out of a tree, gazed at us vaguely and wandered away. I have never felt quite the same about desert islands since. When I went on *Desert Island*

Discs last year, the plumly Plomley was a considerable inprovement on the company of US Marines with whom I had shared Manus. On the other hand, he did censor my choice of luxury – the Marines would have been more sympathetic!

MICHAEL FFOLKES

Wrong Target

In the early days of July 1943 we sailed out into the Mediterranean, on our way to make the first strike into Europe. We were with the American fleet and they landed at Gela/Licata. Not a shot was fired as they made their way up the beach because, with the exception of two Italian policemen, there was no-one there, and so they advanced safely into the countryside.

But soon after that came a disastrous night for the Americans. It was decided there would be a parachute drop by US Rangers toward the north of the island. They were to be flown from North Africa in Dakotas. Many large American warships were at anchor and in the early hours of the morning we were all awakened by the firing of heavy guns. We rushed on deck to find that it was the US cruisers firing into the air. This surprised and puzzled us greatly because the aircraft they were aiming at were coming from the direction of North Africa, territory from which the Allies were operating.

But all hell was let loose up there. Search-lights sliced their way into the night, machine-guns clattered unceasingly and cannon and ack-ack smashed their way into the waves of incoming aircraft. The shocking thing to us was that the pilots seemed reluctant to take evasive action and even when they did so it was with an appalling slowness. So down they came, one after another, twirling, smoking and flaming. Others exploded where they were, leaving nothing to fall but debris. It was a terrifying scene and one that we could only view with near disbelief. What sort of raiders could these be?

A few hours later we learnt the terrible truth: the US warships had shot down 43 of their own Dakotas, each of which carried 50 parachutists. There was not one survivor from any plane, so they succeeded in killing 2,450 of their own men.

JOHN COOK

'Via Rasella: Marisa Italy' from *Women in War*

In July 1943 Mussolini was expelled from office by King Victor Emannuel III and Italy surrendered to the Allies. But German forces overran two-thirds of the country, and it was then that armed partisans began operating throughout Italy.

Approximately ten percent of the partisans were women. In Italy's long and turbulent struggles against foreign occupiers and its own tyrannical rulers, women have always played a role as revolutionaries. Women guerillas are said to have fought for Italy's independence in the mid-nineteenth century, and along the northern borders of the country during World War I. Though denied a role in the Italian armed forces, they have always taken some part in the country's conflicts.

One of the partisans was Marisa Musu, code-named 'Rosa', a mere 18-year-old student in 1943. Since she had been gathering intelligence for the underground since 1941, a sweet shy-looking girl unlikely to arouse suspicion, the progression was a logical one. The group within which she operated went in for sabotage, direct killing of Germans, caring for disbanded soldiers and helping Allied prisoners to hide and escape. The advantage of female operatives was that initially the Germans found it difficult to believe that women could be front-line fighters, and armed at that, so movement was easier for them than for the men.

By 1944 however, they had learned how active the female partisans actually were and Rome became a death-trap, those caught being treated with fearsome barbarism. The tortures they underwent passed belief and those remaining went about their activities in constant dread of capture, knowing that the manner of their death would be agonizing and prolonged. But Marisa stayed with her comrades to torment their occupiers in every way that could be devised.

Yet hopes for a quick Allied victory in Italy were dying. On 16th February 1944 Allied forces landed at Anzio, but German resistance was fierce and fighting continued for three days. Morale was poor in the capital, where constant bombing disrupted public transport, water works and electricity. There were severe food shortages and little heat. The partisans were weakening. They could afford no more than one uncooked meal a day. And still they fought on, infuriating the German command whose own troops were by now becoming demoralized.

So they discussed other means of contending with the partisans. They decided to bring in a specially trained unit to conduct search-and-destroy missions in and just outside Rome. The unit was the 11th Company of the 3rd Bozen Battalion, which consisted of 156 men. They arrived in Rome and began training each day in the city. The partisans observed the unit and noted the time each day when the column marched through the centre of the city as a show of force. The Italian commanders decided on an action that would demonstrate to the Germans they were not intimidated and that they hoped would raise morale among the population. They planned to attack the unit as it crossed the centre of the city one afternoon.

There were some setbacks but the aim was achieved, explosives being planted in a rubbish cart and mortar bombs lobbed in for added weight. Thirty-three men were blown to pieces and another seventy were wounded. They lay amid pools of blood and chunks of concrete, shattered glass and pieces of bodies. The whole area of the city was in chaos. Within minutes truckloads of Germans arrived and began shooting in the streets. Rumours spread that hundreds of people were being shot. SS men began pounding down doors, going from house to house and dragging the inhabitants into the streets. They lined up all the men they found in the area, and with hands forced above their heads the innocent civilians were taken away.

'That same night,' says Marisa. 'the Germans took 330 prisoners from jail – many were the people they had just pulled out of their homes – and they took them to the Ardeatine caves.'

Since they were lying low, knowing they were nearly all identified, she and her fellow-partisans knew nothing of this, nor of the German intentions.

On orders direct from the Fuhrer himself, German commanders in Rome ordered the death of ten Romans for every German killed at Via Rasella. The prisoners were rounded up from jails throughout the city. Some were partisans; most were not. With hands tied behind their backs they were herded into trucks. Any who did not suspect their fate immediately knew it when the trucks screeched into the grounds surrounding the Ardeatine catacombs. German soldiers, numb with alcohol, had lit torches inside the caves. Then, five at a time, the prisoners were led deep inside, forced to kneel against the walls, and were shot in the back of the neck. Night became dawn as the massacre continued, the living forced to climb onto the pile of dead. The Germans sealed up the caves when the night's work was done, and set off explosives.

The partisan hopes of raising Roman morale by their original action was now brought to nothing by the reaction of the Germans. Controversy was rife as the population split into those for and those against the partisans. Even the Pope, whose own war record remains controversial, condemned the partisans: 'Thirty-two (sic) victims on the one hand and on the other three hundred and twenty prisoners (sic) sacrificed for the guilty parties who escaped arrest.' He then called on the people of Rome to stop the violent actions against the Germans.

All of this had some effect, though not total. 'The reprisal made me realize even more strongly that the Germans had to be stopped,' says Marisa. 'I never considered (stopping).'

But of the forty-six actions carried out by the partisans during the ten-month German occupation of Rome, only three occurred after Via Rasella. The civilians, whoever they blamed, were terrified and sickened after the massacre.

SHELLEY SAYWELL

A Visit from the Quality

I was lying on my Charpoy in my Basha in Ceylon, when peace was disturbed by Winco entering and shouting, 'Attention' accompanied by Lady Trefusious fforbes, the first White Lady to come on site. Suddenly Jacko appeared from behind his mosquito net, stark naked and with an erection, as he was reading erotic literature. She took one

look at him, and with a straight face asked me if I was 'happy in the Jungle.' Before I could answer they beat a hasty retreat.

ALAN BELL

Love and War in the Appenines

I woke to find a German soldier standing over me. At first, with the sun behind him he was as indistinct as the peaks had become, but then he swam into focus. He was an officer and he was wearing summer battle-dress and a soft cap with a long narrow peak. He had a pistol but it was still in its holster on his belt and he seemed to have forgotten that he was armed because he made no effort to draw it. Across one shoulder and hanging down over his hip in a very unmilitary way he wore a large old-fashioned civilian haversack, as if he was a member of a weekend rambling club, rather than a soldier, and in one hand he held a large, professional-looking butterfly net. He was a tall, thin, pale young man of about twenty-five with mild eyes and he appeared as surprised to see me as I was to see him, but much less alarmed than I was, virtually immobilised, lying on my back without my boots and socks on.

'Buon giorno,' he said, courteously. His accent sounded rather like mine must, I thought. *'Che bella giornata.'*

At least up to now he seemed to have assumed that I was an Italian, but as soon as I opened my mouth he would know that I wasn't. Perhaps I ought to try and push him over the cliff, after all he was standing with his back to it; but I knew that I wouldn't. It seemed awful to even think of murdering someone who had simply wished me a good day and remarked on what a beautiful one it was, let alone actually doing it. If ever there was going to be an appropriate time to go on stage in the part of the mute from Genoa which I had often rehearsed but never played, this was it. I didn't answer.

'Da dove viene, lei?' he asked.

I just continued to look at him. I suppose I should have been making strangled noises and pointing down my throat to emphasise my muteness, but just as I couldn't bring myself to assail him, I couldn't do this either. It seemed too ridiculous. But he was not to be put off. He removed his haversack, put down his butterfly net, sat down opposite me in the hollow and said:

'Lei, non e Italiano.'

It was not a question. It was a statement of fact which did not require an answer. I decided to abandon my absurd act.

'Si, sono Italiano.'

He looked at me, studying me carefully: my face, my clothes and my boots which, after my accent, were my biggest give-away, although they were very battered now.

'I think that you are English,' he said, finally, in English. 'English, or from one of your colonies. You cannot be an English deserter; you are on the wrong side of the battle front. You do not look like a parachutist or a saboteur. You must be a prisoner of war. That is so, is it not?'

I said nothing.

'Do not be afraid,' he went on. 'I will not tell anyone that I have met you, I have no intention of spoiling such a splendid day either for you or for myself. They are too rare. I have only this one day of free time and it was extremely difficult to organise the transport to get here. I am anxious to collect specimens, but specimens with wings. I give you my word that no one will ever hear from me that I have seen you or your companions if you have any.'

In the face of such courtesy it was useless to dissemble and it would have been downright uncouth to do so.

'Yes, I am English,' I said, but it was sacrifice to admit it. I felt as if I was pledging my freedom.

He offered me his hand. He was close enough to do so without moving. It felt strangely soft when I grasped it in my own calloused and roughened one and it looked unnaturally clean when he withdrew it.

'*Oberleutnant* Frick. Education Officer. And may I have the pleasure of your name, also?'

'Eric Newby,' I said. 'I'm a lieutenant in the infantry, or rather I was until I was put in the bag.' I could see no point in telling him that I had been in SBS, not that he was likely to have heard of it. In fact I was expressly forbidden, as all prisoners were, to give anything but my name, rank and number to the enemy.

'Excuse me? In the bag?'

'Until I was captured. It's an expression.'

He laughed slightly pedantically, but it was quite a pleasant sound. I expected him to ask me when and where I had been captured and was prepared to say Sicily, 1943, rather than 1942, which would have led to all sorts of complications; but he was more interested in the expression I had used.

'Excellent. In the bag, you say. I shall remember that. I have little opportunity now to learn colloquial English. With me it would be more appropriate to say "in the net", or, "in the bottle"; but, at least no one has put you in a prison bottle, which is what I have to do with my captives.'

Although I don't think he intended it to be, I found this rather creepy, but then I was not a butterfly hunter. His English was very good, if perhaps a little stilted. I only wished that I could speak Italian a quarter as well.

He must have noticed the look of slight distaste on my face becuase the next thing he said was, 'Don't worry, the poison is only crushed laurel leaves, a very old way, nothing modern from I.G. Farben.'

Now he began delving in his haversack and brought out two bottles, wrapped in brown paper, which, at first, I thought must contain the laurel with which he used to knock out his butterflies when he caught them; but, in fact, they contained beer, and he offered me one of them.

'It's really excellent beer,' he said. 'Or, at least, I find it so. To my taste Italian beer is not at all good. This is from Munich. Not easy to get now unfortunately. Permit me to open it for you.'

It was cool and delicious. I asked him where he had come from.

'From Salsomaggiore, in the foothills,' he said. 'It is a spa and like all spas it is very melancholy, or at least I find them so, although we Germans are supposed to like melancholy places. It is the feeling that no one who has ever visited them has been quite well, and never will be again, that I find disagreeable. Now it is a headquarters. My job there is to give lectures on Italian culture, particularly the culture of the Renaissance, to groups of officers and any of the men who are interested. It is scarcely arduous because so few of them are.

'I must confess,' he went on, 'that there are some aspects of my countrymen's character that I cannot pretend to understand, I do not speak disloyally to make you feel more friendly to me because, no doubt, you, also, do not always understand your own people, but surely only Germany would employ a professor of entomology from Gottingen with only one lung, whose only interest is *lepidoptera,* to give lectures on Renaissance painting and architecture to soldiers who are engaged in destroying these things as hard as they are able. Do you not think it strange?'

'I wouldn't say that,' I said, 'I'm sure we do the same sort of thing and, if we don't, I'm sure the Americans do.'

'Really,' he said. 'You surprise me. You would not say that it is strange?

'The intention is, of course,' he continued, 'to make us popular with the inhabitants, but that is something we can never be. For instance, I came to that village down there by car. I suggested to the driver that he might like to accompany me up here; but he is not interested in the countryside or *lepidoptera.* Besides he told me that there is a regulation against leaving military vehicles unattended. I did not ask him to accompany me because I wanted his company but because I knew that he would not enjoy himself in that village, or any other. When we arrived at it no one would speak to us. There was scarcely anyone to speak to anyway, which was very strange because it is a Sunday. They must have thought I had come to make some kind of investigation. It might have been better if we had not been wearing guns; but it is a regulation.'

I could visualise the state of panic the village must have been thrown into by their arrival, with the young men running from the houses and the *stalle* and up the mountain-sides, like hunted hares.

'It is not pleasant to be disliked,' he said, 'and it is very unpleasant to be German and to know that one is hated, because one *is* German and, because, collectively, we are wrong in what we are doing. That is why I hate this war, or one of the reasons. And of course, because of this, we shall lose it. We must. We have to.'

'It's going to take you a long time to lose it at this rate,' I said. 'Everything seems to be going very slowly.'

'It may seem so to you,' he said. 'But it won't be here, in Italy, that we shall be beaten. We shall hold you here, at least through this winter and perhaps we could hold you through next summer, but I do not think there will be a next summer. What is going on in Russia is more than flesh and blood can stand. We are on the retreat from Smolensk; we are retreating to the Dnieper. According to people who have just come from there we are losing more men every day than we have lost here in the Italian peninsula in an entire month. And what are you doing?' he asked.

I told him that I was on my way south towards the front. There seemed no point in telling him I was living here. Also I was ashamed.

'If you take the advice of the enemy,' he said, 'you will try to pass the winter here, in these mountains. By the time you get to the battle front it will be very, very cold and very, very difficult to pass through it. Until a few days ago we all thought we would be retiring beyond the Po; but now the winter line is going to be as far south as Rome. It has already been given a name. They call it the *Winterstellung*.'

'Tell me one thing,' I said. 'Where have we got to now. I never hear any news.'

'You have Termoli and Foggia on the east coast, which means that you will now be able to use bombers in close-support and you have Naples; but take my advice and wait for the spring.'

I asked him where he had learned his English. He told me

that he had spent several summer vacations in England before the war.

'I liked England,' he said. 'And the English. You do not work hard but you have the good sense not to be interested in politics. I liked very much your way of life.'

He got to his feet.

'Lieutenant,' he said, 'it has given me great pleasure to have met you. Good luck to you and, perhaps, though I do not think it probable, we shall meet again after the war at Gottingen, or London,'

'Or Philippi,' I felt like saying, but didn't.

'Now if you would be so kind,' he said, 'please give me the empty bottle as I cannot obtain more of this beer without handing the bottles back. Bottles are in short supply.'

The last I saw of him was running across the open downs with his net unfurled, in the direction from which I had come, making curious little sweeps and lunges as he pursued his prey, a tall, thin, rather ungainly figure with only one lung. I was sorry to see him go.

ERIC NEWBY

Invasion Exercise on the Poultry Farm

Softly croons the radiogram, loudly hoot the owls
Judy gives the door a slam and goes to feed the fowls.
Marty rolls a Craven A around her ruby lips
And runs her yellow fingers down her corduroyed hips,
Shuts her mouth and screws her eyes and puffs her fag alight
And hears some most peculiar cries that echo through the
night.

Ting-a-ling the telephone, to-whit to-whoo the owls,
Judy, Judy, Judy girl, and have you fed the fowls?
No answer as the poultry gate is swinging there ajar.
Boom the bombers overhead, between the clouds a star.
And just outside, among the arks, in a shadowy sheltered
place
Lie Judy and a paratroop in horrible embrace.
Ting-a-ling the telephone. 'Yes, this is Marty Hayne.'
'Have you seen a paratroop come walking down your lane?
He may be on your premises, he may be somewhere near,
And if he is report the fact to Major Maxton-Weir.'
White with rage and lined with age but strong and sturdy still
Marty now co-ordinates her passions and her will,
She will teach that Judy girl to trifle with the heart
And go and kiss a paratroop like any common tart.
She switches up the radiogram and covered by the blare
She goes and gets a riding whip and whirls it in the air,
She fetches down a length of rope and rushes, breathing
hard,
To let the couple have it for embracing in the yard.
Crack! the pair are paralysed. Click! they cannot stir
Zip! she's trussed the paratroop. There's no embracing *her*
'Hullo, hullo, hullo, hullo... Major Maxton-Weir?
I've trussed your missing paratroop. He's waiting for you
here.'

JOHN BETJEMAN

Slapton Sands

Large scale rehearsals for D-Day were afoot with all the Allies taking part. This particular practice focused on the actual landings to take place. One group of British landing-craft was concentrated in the Swanage-Studland Bay area, but well out in the Channel, frigates and destroyers were patrolling to ensure that no German E-boats or other craft could slip in and inflict damage. Such security was considered obvious and essential.

At Slapton Sands, however, where the Americans were exercising, the offer of warship support had been declined on the grounds that all was well and there was no possibility of interference from the enemy. What prompted this reasoning at such a delicate stage of the war still remains a mystery, but it ended as it was almost bound to: in carnage.

Before their craft even reached the beach, German E-boats slipped in among them and wrought havoc, there being nothing to stop them. The night was filled with explosions, hails of bullets and the racing engines of the attackers as they struck again and again at the landing-craft and their helpless passengers. In and out they tore and the lumbering vessels could do nothing but take everything that was hurled at them.

When finally they made off into the darkness they had done a bloody and, for them, fruitful job. Of the Americans taking part in the exercise 750 were now dead. It was later estimated that some 400-500 were never found. Many were drowned while still inside their tanks aboard the landing craft, the majority of which carried as many as 30 men and most of which ended up at the bottom of the Channel.

Those who did succeed in reaching the beach were helped by local people, but there were not too many of the latter because large-scale evacuations had been enforced and the inhabitants sent further inland. They did what they could with their depleted numbers, but the task was too great for them and there is no doubt that even more American servicemen perished before aid could arrive.'

A further problem was that the beaches were covered with barbed wire, anti-tank obstacles and even mines. Thus, getting the survivors to the safety of the green grass beyond was, in itself, a perilous operation and further losses were sustained.

As for the E-boats: they simply returned to Northern France without having a single shot fired at them.

Late in 1987 the unveiling of a memorial to the men who died because an officer decided that naval cover was unnecessary took place. Whether or not the officer concerned succeeded in living with his conscience is not known.

There is one other memorial. Within the last couple of years a local Devon man has had one of the Sherman tanks dragged from the waters. It stands lone sentinel above the beach where the tragedy occurred.

JOHN COOK

Aircrew

The grasshopper Wellington comes into land.
The hand on the lever is not my hand.
Mine are more stuck to earth and sand.

Permission to land on the rising ground.
Bandaged the casual aerial wound.
The pub on the hill has change for a pound.

Lying at last on the hugging bed.
The vertical toes and the parallel head.
There was something the girl in the photo said.

Born for a war or born for a game.
The factories are burning, but no one's to blame.
In a thousand years they'll be burning the same.

In the morning they land in the black ages field.
Sun in our air, touch down, and all are concealed.
On an old earth; their sickness will be healed.

BRIAN ALLWOOD
KILLED IN ACTION, 1944

Second Autumn

So here I am
  Upon the German earth, beneath the German sky,
  And birds flock southward, wheeling as they fly,
  And there are morning mists, and trees turn brown,
  And the winds blow, and blow the dead leaves down,
  And lamps are earlier on, and curtains drawn,
  And nights leave frosted dew-drops on the lawn,
  And bonfire smoke goes curling up on high,
Just as on English earth, beneath an English sky.
But here I am.

PATRICK SAVAGE

Those were the Days, my Friend

Having sustained a wound to my leg in 1944 I was placed in a bed in the sick bay, the only patient in a 30-bed room which was unheated, unlit and untended. Three times a day the Company Quartermaster Sergeant, the sole member of the sick bay staff, would cycle half a mile to my sick-bed with my meal. Since it was November, by the time it reached me it was invariably cold and congealed. I could do nothing but suffer it and get down what I could.

The *pièce de résistance,* however, was that the only treatment prescribed by the Medical Officer was that hot cataplasma poultices be applied to the wound twice daily. It so happened that the sick bay and the medical centre were two miles apart. The sick bay attendant would heat the poultices in the centre, then cycle the two miles through thick snow to me, isolated and freezing cold all that way away. I couldn't see that they were doing me all that much good.

Fortunately I was later sent to the local hospital and cured by the newly-available medical wonder: Penicillin. Of course, I had to walk there.

•

On entry to the Army Physical Training Corps we were all subjected to the usual nude inspection by the MO. It was a freezing cold day with snow upon the ground and the rooms were unheated. Every man had to strip completely and line up while we were admitted to the MO's office one by one. As there were about thirty of us I could only feel sorry for any man whose name might chance to begin with Z.

When my turn finally came I marched smartly in, arms and everything else swinging, came to a smart halt and called out my name, followed by 'Sah!'

The MO, no fool to himself, was wrapped up in full dress: uniform, greatcoat, cap, gloves and a scarf. A small one-bar electric fire was drawn so close that it singed the bottom of his coat.

After the full-frontal inspection he told me to turn round. Inadvertently I turned left-wise.

'Don't you know that in the army it's *right*-about-turn?' he screamed at me hysterically, leapt to his feet and promptly burst into flames.

•

During a brief stay at another hospital we were informed that we were to be visited by a very senior officer. The day before the inspection the resident MO, a major, toured the wards and told us that ambulants would stand to attention by their beds. Those not totally bed-patients would sit to attention. *Bed-patients were to lie to attention.*

•

At one stage I was attached as APTC instructor to a Pioneer Corps where those not truly crazy felt duty-bound to act so. One morning I went into the sergeants' mess for breakfast accompanied by several companions. The orderly served us each a three-inch square 'tile', yellowish-brown and quite solid.

'What's this supposed to be?' my neighbour demanded to know.

The circumspect waiter retreated to the kitchen for a consultation with the cook and returned with the answer 'Dried egg, sergeant.'

Immediately my neighbour whipped out his wallet from his top pocket and took from it a stamp and a pen. Sticking the stamp on the egg-tile, he wrote his wife's name and address on one side and on the other the message, 'This was my breakfast this morning.'

•

At one Pioneer Depot the Camp Games Officer decided to clear away a tree which encroached upon the football pitch, (actually a rough field). A dozen Pioneers launched an assault upon trunks and roots, but their efforts were to no avail so the officer ordered the boring of a small hole and the laying of a charge. This too was carried out yet even this detonation did nothing to loosen the well-entrenched roots.

By now the officer was growing angry. He was not going to be defeated by a mere tree, so there was only one thing for it: a larger charge was needed. The one he laid was a beauty, so much so that when the fuse was lit everyone donned their steel helmets and retired as far away as possible.

When the explosion occurred it did so with all the apparent force of a V2 rocket causing everyone in the camp to come running: cooks, clerks, even company commanders, to find out what the hell had hit them.

What they found was one completely demolished tree, plus one enormous crater in the football field, plus every single window within range totally shattered.

The Games Officer was posted.

•

At one army camp it was necessary to site both soldiers and girls of the ATS. Naturally, any possible mixing of the sexes could not be countenanced so the men were sited to one end of the camp and the girls at the other, with the middle left empty. It was a sad situation however, as the summer was hot which meant that the girls liked to sunbathe. The men not only had eyes but also field glasses as well, so things were not as bad as they could have been. In fact some of the sights were quite uplifting.

Then a terrible thing happened: the powers-that-be decided not only to billet German POWs in the camp but to put them in the middle section. This alone was bad enough but immediately instructions were issued in Part II Company Orders that on no account were any of the ATS to sunbathe in bras and knickers for fear of being seen by the Germans and doubtless corrupting them.

The joy went from life and field glasses became redundant over night. As can be readily understood, resentment of the POWs turned to open hostility and their stay was short.

•

Toward the end of the war I was stationed at a camp which was used as an Army Convalescent Depot. There soldiers recovering from wounds, operations or illnesses would attend for remedial exercises comparable with physiotherapy, supervised by doctors but instructed by APTC staff. Conditions were quite out of the ordinary for the army: food was good and plentiful, there were cinema shows, educational classes, lectures on a wide variety of topics, walks, a pub next to the camp gates and dances every weekend with girls bussed in on 3-tonners.

For those not in too much distress, life could scarcely have been better, but there was one constant threat in this idyllic existence: every fortnight the patients were examined on their progress in recovery by a doctor and an APTC instructor. As they improved the colour-flash worn on their epaulettes was changed. In itself this meant little to them until the final fortnight of their stay approached. Then the light would dawn upon them as they realised they were on the brink of being Returned To Unit.

This was something to be avoided at all costs so they would begin to find the increasingly weighted activities too difficult to cope with. When the screw on the back wheel of the stationary bicycle was tightened a little more they didn't have the strength to pedal, weights were impossible to lift and running laps around the parade-ground was too taxing on their respiration.

All the dodges were quite familiar to the APTC staff and sarcasm would become common currency. But we would patiently wait for them to drive the final nails into their own coffins. This invariably happened at the weekend dances when what should happen but the poor crippled things would make a full and complete recovery as they hurled themselves and their partners about the floor in the jive and boogie-woogie, many of then going into the strangest contortions imaginable.

It was difficult for them to deny their fitness at the next remedial class.

•

There is too the apocryphal story of the sergeant storming into the privates' dormitory shouting, 'Come on then, you dozy lot, let's 'ave you on the grass ahtside! We've got a learned man who's gonna talk to you abaht Keats – and I'll bet not one of you knows what a Keat is!'

•

The NAAFI at one camp where I was stationed was the only on-camp venue where the lowest ranks could meet for a chat, play cards or dominoes, or even get something to eat and drink. As the last meal of the day was tea at 4.30 most of the men would go there at night for a mug of tea and a 'wad' of cake. Those possessed of more cash could buy a hot meal, invariably something basic like sausage and chips or pie and chips.

There was always a great deal of ribald banter between the soldiers and the NAAFI girls, mostly funny and often vulgar, though the girls took it all in good part.

This particular night I was waiting for my mate, Bert. On the menu was just one hot meal. It had been chalked on a blackboard which was placed on the counter facing the men. It read:

RISSOLES
and
CHIPS

Some wag had rubbed out the rear leg of the 'R' so that it became a 'P'.

In came Bert and with a perfectly straight face said to the girl behind the counter, 'I'll have pissholes and chips, please, love.'

This was too much even for her. 'What do you mean?' she asked in disgust.

Bert turned the board toward her. 'That's what it says here.'

'That 'P' should be an 'R', she cried.

'Alright then,' Bert shrugged. 'I'll have arseholes and chips.'

HARRY PLATT AND KEN PARSONS

Dabs & Flounders

The defaulter's offence was a punishable one and he well knew it, so he finished his lame excuse then added the impassioned cry, 'And it's true, as God's my judge – I'm not guilty!'

The OC's response was swift and final. 'He isn't. I am. You are. Twenty eight days' detention.'

•

Signing for his pay, the recruit found difficulty with the now almost blunt pencil he'd picked up from the table. The sergeant behind him ordered, 'Put your weight on it!'

So he did – all twelve and a half stone of it.

•

The blackout was complete and the soldier on picket duty was cold, fed up and needed a smoke, so he took the risk and

lit up. No sooner had he done so than there came the sound of approaching footsteps.

'Halt, who goes there?' he shouted into impenetrable darkness.

'Orderly Officer,' came the reply. 'Give me an order!'

In total panic the guard stubbed his fag out, but took too long about it.

'Don't keep me standing here all night!'

Oh God, what to say? 'Orderly Officer, stand at ease.'

•

After successfully applying for a leave pass over several week-ends, the soldier again explained that his wife was (still) expecting.

'What's she expecting now?' the officer asked wearily.

'She's expecting me back there, as always,' was the answer.

•

The regimental paymaster's officer received a letter from an intake's wife. It read, 'I'm sending here my twins' birth certificate.' A spelling error had been corrected on it. 'One of them is a mistake as you can see, so please make the necessary allowances as soon as possible.'

•

Came a letter to the regimental paymaster's office asking urgently for help towards essential clothing. 'My husband serves with your battalion but doesn't allow me enough for myself and his children. I've no money for clothes and have to keep asking the chapel here locally. Without things to wear I'm relying on visits from them at times and have to face continuing embarrassment.'

•

The matelot was lounging against the guard rails when a lieutenant appeared behind him. 'Shouldn't a conscripted rating know that eight bells have gone? Answer me, man.'

'Suppose so,' the conscript replied, looking idly about him. 'But you can't leave anything safely on this deck, can you?'

ANON

from *'Women in War'*

Jeanne began intensive training immediately. At a school in the countryside she was tested physically, with strenuous physical exercises, including running and jumping over ditches and walls. She underwent mental testing, practised memorization and problem solving in specified scenarios and was taught Morse code. Then she was sent to a sabotage school in Scotland, where she was the only female. 'They made me sleep in separate quarters and eat with the instructors. I couldn't do physical exercises with the others.' Weapons training included pistols and revolvers, and the Sten sub-machine gun that was the mainstay of the Resistance fighters. 'I was clumsy at first, but eventually was as good as the others,' she claims. She learned instinctive shooting, which involves a quick reaction rather than careful aiming, and tested this in a room where moving silhouettes represented the enemy. There were courses on explosives, using jelly-plastic detonators and delayed-action devices.

'We had even more original courses,' she later wrote in *La plastiqueuse à bicyclette*. ' "How to be the perfect burglar." A cockney taught the course and I had the feeling that he had genuine experience. He taught us how to open locks without keys. We also learned everything on "silent killing." It was a mixture of karate, close combat and the use of daggers. We learned how to put someone out or even kill them with bare-fisted blows. This training left me sceptical about my own chances against a determined and strong man, but perhaps someone caught off guard would find it hard to beat me. In any case the apprenticeship gave us confidence in our potential, and fighting spirit that would be essential to us.'

SHELLEY SAYWELL

Never Try to be Clever with the Army

In 1945 I was a clerk in the Royal Engineers, serving in Capua in the South of Italy. One day I attended a meeting where we discussed a building project which had become the subject of some emotion. Somebody complained that certain window frames, supplied from the UK, were too small for requirements.

It was plain to me that a young officer was responsible, that he had ordered the wrong size, and was now attempting a 'cover up'. He was asked to explain why the window frames were two inches too small.

The Second Lieutenant told us that throughout the south of Europe there is a condition of extreme humidity and that therefore substances like timber are liable to shrink.

A disbelieving silence followed this audacious statement and then a humble sapper asked permission to put a question. This being granted, he said:

'If I had a piece of wood which was two inches square, and I brought it here, would it disappear?'

The Sergeant Major intervened:

'Take that man's name, Corporal.'

I expect he was charged under the Army Act as having shown a lack of respect.

I can no longer remember the young officer's name but suspect that later he may have found his true vocation as a cabinet minister.

WILLIAM E. LEE

Military Manoeuvre

Lieutenant Tommy Thomas had twin desires. One, to continue the celebration of VE day in a state of inebriation until demob and two, to hasten his posting to the UK by all possible means, fair or foul.

In pursuit of his first aim he had no problem, but the fixing of his home posting was proving surprisingly elusive. However, he had a plan. He figured that incompetence in the field was something his CO wouldn't just brush aside, and it might succeed in getting him on that 'big boat' where drunkenness and insubordination had failed so miserably.

News of full-scale manoeuvres would normally have filled Tommy with an impenetrable gloom, but on the morning of VE plus 62 he received the information with unalloyed joy, if not euphoria. Here was a heaven-sent opportunity to expose his inefficiency – 'in spades'.

The evening of VE plus 61 had been celebrated with more than usual gusto, and Tommy was still boozed-up when he arrived on his gun position. His orders were to fire a smoke-screen for the advancing infantry led by Colonel Whitton, a fiery officer late of the Indian Army, which in any other circumstances he would have considered both irksome and futile. Now, however, he was full of the joy of anticipation. His master-plan was ready.

The guns were loaded with 'smoke' and made ready to fire. Tommy shambled around the Command Post, hip flask firmly clasped in one hand and the tannoy in the other. He was glassy-eyed and looked half asleep, but the sound of his Battery Commander giving the firing orders galvanised him into action.

Abandoning the decorum required of an officer and a gentleman, and casting aside the hallowed precepts of the Training Manual, he pressed the tannoy button and yelled, 'When you're ready lads, let 'em *all* go.'

The full complement of 'smoke' from *four* guns whistled over the horizon. Tommy became hysterical. He leapt about like a Zulu warrior to the unconcealed delight of his men, and the acute embarrassment of his junior officer. His delight knew no bounds. When he received a message on the 'blower' from his BC saying that Colonel Whitton would see him in the Mess immediately after the end of the exercise, he just laughed. He imagined Whitton purple with rage. This time he really had fixed it. Already he could see himself striding up the gang-plank in Alex.

When it seemed in the bag, however, Fate struck a cruel blow.

Colonel Whitton was ecstatic when Tommy met him in the Mess. He declared that the smokescreen was the best his men had ever had the privilege to walk under and hailed Tommy as the hero of the hour. Instead of emasculation in the Army tradition, everyone wanted to buy him a drink and toast the Colonel's blue-eyed boy.

Tommy knew how to milk a situation. He had a feeling that VE plus 62 was going to be an evening he would remember for the rest of his life. There was no point in bearing malice. Blighty would have to wait.

That evening, reclining in a club chair behind an extra large whisky, Tommy lifted his glass in salute to a new friend.

'First to-day, Colonel,' he chuckled, ' – in this glass.'

GEOFFREY W. HARTLEY

After the Final Victory

Shen Kuo-hwa, the little guerilla boy, stood by my table, relating an exciting story about the battle of Machiachung three weeks before, when the Japanese had attacked the guerilla base. During the retreat of the guerillas, a bullet had passed through his upper arm and he had been in the hospital for two weeks.

He was ten years old. Standing entirely naked by my table, he seemed much frailer and smaller than any Chinese boy of ten. His thin, wistful face was turned up to mine. Behind him stood the small wooden tub in which he had just bathed, and near by was a brazier of gleaming charcoal. He was waiting for me to delouse his uniform, which was his only suit of clothing. He had no underclothing at all, but I had bought a shirt for him. While he talked, I would thrust the charcoal tongs in among the gleaming charcoal and while they heated, I would wet the inside seam of the uniform. Then, as I drew the hot tongs down the seams, the steam would arise and the lice would crack.

'It won't take much longer,' I told him, 'for you are small.' And I looked at him to see how he would take this remark.

'I'm small because I never had enough to eat, and because I was sick so much when I was a beggar boy.'

'You're not so very big just now, but later on you will be a big strapping fellow. Then what will you do?'

'I want to ride a horse and fight the Japanese devils.' He spoke solemnly.

While the tongs were heating again I bent over and examined the deep red scar on his arm.

'That happened when we were crossing the highway,' he explained again. 'We had many killed and wounded men in the battle. But we captured three of the devils. One was in the hospital with me. He was afraid at first, but we treated him well and then he was not afraid.

'Look,' the child said, lifting one leg and showing another scar. 'That's where a dog bit me. When I was a beggar boy people used to set their dogs on me. I am always afraid of dogs. I think they are going to eat me.' He was a small, fearful child when he spoke of dogs.

'Ai-yoh – but your uniform is filled with lice!' I exclaimed.

'Every one has lice in winter. Some orderlies have more than I.'

'Lice are very dangerous. They give you dangerous diseases.'

'Yes. Men often die here from louse sickness. One died yesterday, and then all the lice crawled off his body – he had many, *very* many.'

'Was he in hospital?'

'The hospital is too far away.'

'Where was he when he died?'

'He lay on some straw.'

'Did a doctor take care of him?'

'We have no doctor here. But the soldiers gave him water and food when he wanted anything.'

I deloused the uniform and thought – of delousing stations to prevent typhus and relapsing fever. But the guerilla detachment moved often, for Japanese garrisons were all about it and there was almost continual fighting. I looked down at the child and asked:

'Do you think you can keep free of lice? The reason men are dying is because of lice.'

'In the army there is no way. We all sleep together to keep warm. When I am with you, it is all right. When you go, I will get lice again. Even when I was very small, before I joined the army, I had lice in the winter time. I used to watch them. There are two kinds of lice – red lice and white lice. When they are babies they have two legs only.'

'When they crawl on me I think they have a million legs.'

'That's because you have only a few. Then you itch. If you

get many lice you don't itch; you just get a headache and we call it louse sickness. Many other orderlies like me have a headache all the time.'

'Come now, get into your clothing. If you feel any tomorrow I will do it again. Tonight I will boil your shirt and then you can put it on.'

The child put on his uniform, then solemnly and gratefully said, 'You are both my father and my mother.'

I drew him to me, held him between my knees and combed his hair.

'Where did you get this big scar on your cheek?' I asked.

'When I was very small, bandits burned down our house and killed my father and injured my mother. I was burned then.'

While we talked a Chinese woman reporter who was with me in the guerilla detachment came in, with another little boy, who was her orderly. We were soon busy delousing the boy. The two children kept up an excited patter about this unusual event, about their daily lives, about the classes they attended each day where they learned to read and write. Often it was difficult to get them to act like children with us because the army had given them orderly work and they acted like little men. They cleaned our rooms in the morning, brought tea or water for washing, and kept our fires burning. Because we were guests, we had a charcoal fire. But the guerillas were too poor to buy charcoal for others. It was winter time and the snow lay on the ground. The wind swished past our paper-covered windows. Our rooms were the only ones warm enough for a bath.

'What a miserable existance! This storm is miserable!' the woman reporter exclaimed, listening to the wind.

Shen Kuo-hwa was peering through a hole in the paper window. 'The storm will not last long,' he told her. 'When the wind sounds like that and the snow lies like that on the ground, the snow will soon stop.'

'How do you know?' she asked.

'When I tended cows for the big landlord I watched the snow and listened to the wind each winter. Before that I watched, too, for I was a beggar boy.'

'When and where was all that?'

'In Honan, before I joined this army, I worked for a landlord for three years. My mother asked a small landlord to guarantee me to a big landlord, so I got a job tending cows. The landlord paid me eighty cents a year. Yes, he gave me food. If his sons threw away any clothing he gave some to me. My mother used my eighty cents to make me shoes for winter.'

'How old were you?' The woman's voice was as sad as the wind outside.

'I was six when I got the job.'

'How long were you a beggar boy?'

'I think it was two years. It was before I tended cows. It was after the bandits burned our home and killed my father and injured my mother. My two brothers had joined the army to make a living. So we had nothing. Then my mother told me to beg. She said I must find a rich man's house and beg before it. I was very little and I did not know how to beg. But I found a big house and many people went in and came out all day. I stood there all day but no one saw me. When it was dark a man who had gone in and come out many times saw me and told me to go home; he said all children ought to be in bed. I told him the bandits had burned our house and we had no bed and no food. Then he gave me a little money and I went to find my mother. After that I was a beggar boy for two years. It was very bad. People treat you very badly; they used to set their dogs on me and drive me away. I was sick very much.'

'What did you do when you were sick?'

'I would find a place and lie down.'

The delousing had finished and as he talked the child was

leaning against me. Now he lowered his head and was silent. The bill of his small military cap hid his face. He made no motion and no sound, but tears were rolling down his cheeks and falling on my jacket. I lifted his chin in my hand and wiped the tears away. The other little orderly watched us, then said cheerfully: 'Kuo-hwa is a very good orderly and makes no trouble with the other orderlies. He studies hard and has learned to read and write a lot.'

This simple tribute caused Kuo-hwa to look gratefully at the other boy. He ceased crying. But he was a child so humble that he could not take credit for even learning to read and write.

'The army taught me,' he replied. 'Before I joined the army I tried to learn, but no one would teach me. I used to watch rich boys go to school with their book satchels. I learned to write the characters for one, two and three, but four and five were very hard and I could not get any one to help me. I asked a man once, but he pushed me and asked me what a beggar boy wanted to learn to read and write for. He said, "Get out!" But I learned to write "quality" because it is on boxes of goods before shops and it has three squares. I learned how to write "matches" and the name of the firm that makes matches. I would write with a stick or my finger, in the dust. But no one ever taught me to write my name. I learned that in the army. But I don't know much yet.'

The other little orderly defended him stoutly: 'I think he knows over two hundred characters,' he told us. 'Of course I know more because I am older and have been in the army longer. Kuo-hwa learns quickly. He is the best orderly in the army.'

'You are a good orderly, too, and very willing,' Kuo-hwa replied.

The woman reporter looked from one child to the other, her face eloquent with tenderness.

'How did you get into this army?' she asked Kuo-hwa.

'Wang Lao-han brought me. He is a good man. One day my brother's army came to Choshan on the Pinghan railway. My brother saw my mother begging on the streets, but he would not give her any money. My good brother was killed in the battle of Lukouchiao (Marco Polo Bridge). This bad brother said I was a fool for working for a landlord for eighty cents a year. He said I ought to get a good job that paid good money.

'While my brother's army was in Choshan I heard some soldiers talking. They said the Eighth Route Army was a poor man's army, every one learned how to read and write, and officers could not beat the soldiers. But they said the soldiers were paid only one dollar and a half a month. I thought I would join the Eighth Route Army, and I asked the soldiers where I could find it. They laughed and said it was far away. I asked a policeman where I could find it, but he said it was made up of bandits and he shook me by the arm and asked me why I wanted to find it. I said it was the poor man's army and I was a poor man.'

'Never ask a policeman anything!' the other little orderly cautioned.

'After that, what did you do?' the woman reporter asked Kuo-hwa.

'Once in Choshan I saw an old man with a beard and a kind face, and though he was old he had on a military uniform. I asked him the same question, and he smiled and patted me on the head and said the Eighth Route Army was very far away and I was too small to join an army. I followed him and told him how I could walk and work, and how the landlord's servants sometimes beat me and made me do their work too. I followed him all day. His name was Wang Lao-han, and he was from this New Fourth Army Storm Guerilla Detachment. He said it was a poor man's army, too, but it did not have enough food and clothing and could not pay much money.

'Wang Lao-han did not want me to follow him but when he went to a village outside Choshan he got tired of saying I must go back. Then I came with him here.'

The storm ceased, but the snow lay in great drifts on the mountain paths. At such a time there would be no fighting. So the woman reporter sat by the fire in my room, a small boy on either side of her, and they talked. The boys brought their small pocket manuals, and she helped them study. While I wrote at the table, their low, soft voices filled the room like gentle music. Listening, sometimes I heard them drilling: 'I am a human being. You are a human being. He is a human being.' Then they would look at the bottom of the page for the discussion theme and read. 'Why is there a distinction between the rich and the poor among human beings?' They would read further, 'The peasants grow rice.' And the discussion theme: 'Why can workers and peasants not consume the things they produce?' Or they would discuss: 'Why is reliance on another man unreliable?' 'Why are the rich and the poor both anti-Japanese today?' 'Why is Japanese imperialism the most ruthless in the world?'

The snow along the mountain paths became packed hard by the marching feet of soldiers. And one day the woman reporter and I returned to our rooms. 'We are going with the regiment in to the lake region,' we told the boys. 'When we return you can be our orderlies again.'

Kuo-hwa stood with lowered head. He was a little soldier and seemed to be taking an order obediently, silently. Humble, he expected little, and was grateful that the guerillas had allowed him to share their barren, dour life.

'Kuo-hwa,' I said. 'Can you keep free of lice while I am gone?'

'No,' he replied. 'There is no way. We must all sleep close together to keep warm.'

'How far have you walked in the army?'

'Sometimes we march all night, in the dark, and I carry

things like the others. I could go with you –' then he lowered his head and said dully – 'if you want me.'

The woman reporter and I looked at each other. Did we dare take these children into a region of great danger? The Children's Dramatic Corps was already in that region, she insisted. I thought of Kuo-hwa remaining here, where relapsing fever killed men each day.

'Kuo-hwa – we will ask permission for you both to come with us. We leave late this afternoon. Can you get ready?'

The child lifted his face to ours and both boys began talking eagerly. 'We can always be ready in five minutes,' they assured us.

Then the woman reporter and I, and our two small orderlies, went into the lake region near Hankow. And in going there, the armed escort with which we marched came suddenly face to face with the Japanese, and fought. The midnight darkness was split with the singing of bullets and the bursting of hand-grenades, and those of us who were not fighters were told to run quickly behind the shelter of hills. Kuo-hwa, the woman reporter, my secretary and two new volunteers without guns found themselves in one group, and none knew where I was. Kuo-hwa then began running about in the darkness, asking desperately if the devils had caught me. He told the others that he could go out into the night and shout, and that I would answer his voice, but that I would fear to answer any one else lest it be a Japanese devil.

The woman reporter took him by the hand and told him to remain silent because he was a child and could not find me.

Angrily he turned on her and said: 'When she came to our army, they told me to serve her and they said I was responsible for her. It is my duty to the army to find and protect her!'

But when they all refused to allow him to venture into the darkness to find me, the little soldier became a sobbing child. They pitied him and said he could never find his way back.

Once more he became the soldier. He ceased crying, looked at the encircling hills, at a few trees, and then for a long time at the stars above.

'I can find her and bring her back to this place,' he stated.

Yet they refused. Later, when we all had assembled once more, the child came quickly to my side and placed his hands on my arm.

Knowing what he had tried to do, I said to him: 'Yes – you were right; I would have answered you, but no one else.' And then he was quiet and at peace. Often my impulse was to put my arms about him and comfort him. Always I hesitated, not knowing the effect. A bitter life had fashioned him into a small creature that lived within himself, alone. In the army there was comradeship in ideas and in general struggle, but each person – man or child – had to care for himself or fall behind in the march of life. Even the reading textbooks contained the discussion topic: 'Why is reliance on another person unreliable?' Already my contact with this small life had disturbed a pattern that had been laid and I could not say if it was for the better.

In the weeks that followed, the woman reporter and I always found time to write in our notebooks. Kuo-hwa would often come up and stand watching us in silence. Once he asked us what we wrote, and then the woman reporter read to him and explained that we wrote not just what we saw, but what men said, and sometimes what we ourselves felt and thought.

Then we saw that the child was trying to do as we did. He would take any bit of paper or open a cast-off cigarette case and write on the inside of it. He would sit thinking, wet the lead of his pencil on his tongue and write; then think again. Once I picked up such a case and asked the woman reporter to read to me what he had written. She read these words:

'Got up before the sun and walked on hill. Fog everywhere in trees. Sun came up big and red and fog went away. Went down hill and saw Wang Lao-han coming. I felt glad. But he forgot me and forgot he brought me to army. I feel sad. I went away.'

Soon the time came when I had to leave the guerilla army. For weeks I had thought of the problem of Kuo-hwa. If he remained in the army, he would receive some education, but it would be limited. From the rank of orderly he would later become a guard, from a guard a soldier, and from the rank of soldier he would become a commander. If he lived! But his body was too frail to withstand a dangerous disease. And, it seemed to me, in him were rare qualities. With the woman reporter I discussed a special school in western China, where life was simple and even austere, yet where the children were well-fed and well-clothed, where they did their own work, but where serious emphasis was laid on the teaching of science. Then I went to the commander and asked if I could adopt Kuo-hwa.

'Oh, of course,' the commander replied, 'if the boy is willing. But why choose him?'

'Because he has watched the growth of lice, the way the wind blows, the way the snow drifts, the position of stars at night. He has given the stars names of his own. And he can describe well what he sees and thinks in writing.'

A number of men, listening, smiled, and one said. 'I can do all those things also.' The commander's eyes narrowed and he remarked dryly: 'So can I. What about adopting us also?' And a burly fellow leaning against the door added: 'I know more about lice than your little devil Kuo-hwa. I don't know if I can write as well, but I have many other strong points.'

That night the woman reporter and I talked with Kuo-hwa and told him about the school. He feared going among 'rich little boys,' but we told him it was not that kind of school. 'You can come back to the army later and teach what you have learned,' we urged. He said he would talk with the other little orderly and tell me the next day. And the next morning the two of them came, and Kuo-hwa gave his decision, from which we could not move him.

'We think all men must remain at the front,' he said. 'You can adopt me after the final victory.'

AGNES SMEDLEY

The Veterans

You ask us why we do it,
Why do we still parade.
When we are getting older
And just a little frayed.

It's not for the sake of glory,
Or the medals on our chest;
It's simply we are comrades,
Who stood to face the test.

The world we knew when we were young,
Was full of grief and pain,
We were filled with great ideals,
To put it right again.

We wanted peace, not just for us
But all the world as well,
And so that day upon the beach
We entered the jaws of hell.

History will tell you,
Of the things we had to do,
To win that peace for the world,
And our Mother Country, too.

Like knights of old campaigning,
We wore Crusaders Cross –
The British Second Army –
But we suffered grievous loss.

On June the sixth, that fateful day,
A day we'll not forget,
Many a lad laid down his life
And paid the final debt.

What we did in Europe,
Gave to the world new hope,
We put an end to tyranny,
When others couldn't cope.

Yes, we brought peace to Europe,
A peace that's lasting still,

It was no easy road to travel
And we climbed a mighty hill.

So when you see a veteran,
Give the man your hand.
The medals you see upon his chest,
Were won on a foreign strand.

This man may be old in years,
And yet his heart is free;
He knows the things that he did,
He did for you and me.

This man earned the glory,
He also knew much pain;
Yet should his country need him,
He would do it all again.

When the last rally is sounded,
And we answer the final call,
In the presence of our Maker
We shall feel rather small.

But when God asks the question,
'Who are you, my man?'
Then I will proudly answer,
'Sir, I am a veteran.'

TOM SANDS, CHAIRMAN
D-DAY AND NORMANDY VETERANS ASSOCIATION, PUDSEY (FOUNDER)
BRANCH, WEST YORKSHIRE

from *Sword of Honour*
Epilogue:
Festival of Britain

In 1951, to celebrate the opening of a happier decade, the government declared a Festival. Monstrous constructions appeared on the south bank of the Thames, the foundation stone was solemnly laid for a National Theatre, but there was little popular exuberance among the straitened people and dollar-bearing tourists curtailed their visits and sped to the countries of the Continent where, however precarious their condition, they ordered things better.

There were few private parties. Two of these were held in London on the same June evening.

Tommy Blackhouse had returned to England in May. He was retiring from the army with many decorations, a new, pretty wife and the rank of major-general. In the last year he had advanced far beyond his commando into posts of greater and greater eminence and responsibility, never seeming to seek promotion, never leaving rancour behind him among those he surpassed; but his first command lay closest to his heart. Meeting Bertie in Bellamy's he had suggested a reunion dinner. Bertie agreed that it would be agreeable. 'It would mean an awful lot of organizing though,' said this one-time adjutant. It was left for Tommy, as always, to do the work.

The officers who had assembled at Mugg were not so scattered as those of other war-time units. Most of them had been together in prison. Luxmore had made an escape. Ivor Claire had spent six months in Burma with the Chindits, had done well, collected a DSO and an honourably incapacitating wound. He was often in Bellamy's now. His brief period of disgrace was set aside and almost forgotten.

'You're going to invite everyone?' asked Bertie.

'Everyone I can find. What was the name of that old

Halberdier? Jumbo someone? We'll ask the sea-weed eater. I don't somehow think he'll come. Guy Crouchback of course.'

'Trimmer?'

'Certainly' But Trimmer had disappeared. All Tommy's adroit enquiries failed to find any trace of him. Some said he had jumped ship in South Africa. Nothing was known certanly. Fifteen men eventually assembled including Guy.

The second, concurrent festivity was given in part by Arthur Box-Bender. He had lost his seat in parliament in 1945. He rarely came to London in the succeeding years but that June evening he was induced to pay his half share in a small dance given in an hotel for his eighteen-year-old daughter and a friend of hers. For an hour or two he stood with Angela greeting the ill-conditioned young people who were his guests. Some of the men wore hired evening-dress; others impudently presented themselves in dinner-jackets and soft shirts. He and his fellow-host had been at pains to find the cheapest fizzy wine in the market. Feeling thirsty, he sauntered down Piccadilly and turned into St James's. Bellamy's alone retained some traces of happier days.

Elderberry was alone in the middle hall reading Air Marshal Beech's reminiscences. He, also, had lost his seat. His successful opponent, Gilpin, was not popular in the House but he was making his mark and had lately become an under-secretary. Elderberry had no habitation outside London. He had no occupation there. Most of his days and evenings were passed alone in this same armchair in Bellamy's.

He looked disapprovingly at Box-Bender's starched front.

'You still go out?'

'I had to give a party tonight for my daughter.'

'Ah, something you had to pay for? That's different. It's being asked I like. I'm never asked anywhere now.'

'I don't think you would have liked this party.'

'No, no, of course not. But I used to get asked to dinners – embassies and that kind of thing. Well, so did you. There was a lot of rot talked but it did get one through the evening. Everything's very quiet here now.'

This judgment was immediately rebutted by the descent of the Commando dinner party who stumbled noisily down the staircase and into the billiard room.

Guy paused to greet his brother-in-law.

'I didn't ask you to our dance,' said Box-Bender, 'It is very small, for young people. I didn't suppose you'd want to come. Didn't know you ever came to London as a matter of fact.'

'I don't, Arthur. I'm just up to see the lawyers. We've sold the Castello, you know.'

'I'm glad to hear it. Who on earth can afford to buy property in Italy now? Americans, I suppose.'

'Not at all. One of our own countrymen who can't afford to live in England – Ludovic.'

'Ludovic?'

'The author of *The Death Wish.* You must have heard of it.'

'I think Angela read it. She said it was tosh.'

'It sold nearly a million copies in America and they've just filmed it. He's a fellow I came across during the war.'

'One of your party in there?'

'No. We aren't quite Ludovic's sort of party.'

Well, the Castello should be just the place for a literary man. Clever of you to find a buyer.'

'That was done for me by another fellow I met in the war. You may remember him. An American called Padfield. He used to belong here. He's become Ludovic's factotum now.'

'Padfield? No. Can't say I remember him. How's everything at Broome?'

'Very well, thank you.'

'Domenica all right, and the children?'

'Yes'.

'Farm paying?'

'At the moment.'

'Wish mine was. Well, give them all my regards.' A voice called, 'Guy, come and play slosh.'

'Coming, Bertie.'

When he had gone, Elderberry said: 'That's your brother-in-law, isn't it? He's putting on weight. Didn't I hear something rather sad about him during the war?'

'His wife was killed by a bomb.'

'Yes, that was it. I remember now. But he's married again?'

'Yes. The first sensible thing he's ever done. Domenica Plessington, Eloise's girl. Eloise looked after the baby while Guy was abroad. Domenica got very fond of it. A marriage was the obvious thing. I think Eloise deserves some credit in arranging it. No children of their own, but that's not always a disadvantage. Domenica manages the home farm at Broome. They've settled in the agent's house. They aren't at all badly off. Angela's uncle Peregrine left his little bit to the child. Wasn't such a very little bit either.'

Elderberry remembered that Box-Bender had had trouble with his own son. What had it been? Divorce? Debt? No, something odder than that. He'd gone into a monastery. With unusual delicacy Elderberry did not raise the question. He merely said: 'So Guy's happily settled?'

'Yes,' said Box-Bender, not without a small, clear note of resentment, 'things have turned out very conveniently for Guy.'

EVELYN WAUGH

Across the River and Into the Ritz

Twenty years ago this week, everyone in the Paris area was liberating everyone and everything. General Leclerc, at the head of the Second French armoured division, has had his gesture of liberation recorded for posterity in a photograph which in the French Communist press carries a fresh interpretation that Leclerc is being greeted by the Parisian people who had liberated themselves.

Meanwhile, General Patton was fondling his pearl-handled revolvers and riding in on the tide of victory with the not too young but troublesomely energetic Ernest Hemingway, scouting ahead near Rambouillet, in a white-washed Citroen, from which he had torn the doors to facilitate quick exit. Some say that the American army had given Hemingway carte blanche to press on ahead in the hope that he would get his ears shot off, and stop making a bedlam of the press conference. Among the proudest of the advance guard hard on Hemingway's heels were the occupants of the converted Humber ambulance housing the BBC French recording unit, which during the war in the programme 'Les Francaise parlent aux Francais' had encouraged the French not to lose hope.

Pierre Lefevre, the young commentator who in those days before tape recorders registered his exhilarated impression of the triumphant advance of this tragic, comic cavalcade on a portable gramophone, crouching on the roof of the ambulance, and who finally liberated the Ritz hotel with Hemingway, is now a well-known producer/actor of the Comedie de L'Est in Strasbourg. Like a lot of Frenchmen this week, he is reliving those days with relish and nostalgia.

'Michel St Denis, at the head of the programme, had sent us out secretly to join Leclerc whose objective was Paris,' M. Lefevre told us in a nicely preserved BBC accent. 'Leclerc found us a bit unorthodox, and was not too pleased, but with Hemingway with us we managed to get around this. I had met Hemingway when we got to Monte St Michele. He was writing for the *Saturday Evening Post* and already in bad odour with General Patton. I think that was why they gave him carte blanche; to get him out of the way. He had his own little commando of eight young fellows from the Maquis, wearing insignia "HEM GI," and a rough-necked American sergeant to keep an eye on him. The first thing he did was rope us in, Sammy Sampson, the BBC recording engineer and myself to go out and liberate a dyke near the Monte St Michele. In fact there was noboby there, but if there had been we could have been cleaned-up out in the open like that. Hemingway liked to do that kind of thing.'

'They say he was very reckless?'

'He was very tough, and very affectionate. He always had to have a pal. He wanted company; he was that sort of chap. I happened to be around so I became his friend for a few days. At Monte St Michele he woke us up in the morning at our hotel and produced a bottle of wine saying. "Breakfast is ready." He had his wild beard, of course, and tremendous energy. With his little band of commandos he was really playing at being a general.' M Lefevre laughed at the image it conjured up. 'He was a nice fellow.'

'He was of course the *enfant terrible* of the war correspondents, and very much the senior in years and experience. Sampson and I were the youngest and most green, but we managed to collect quite a lot of good recordings of what was going on. Our van was a bit conspicuous out there in the advance guard; we had to go out ahead with a microphone and record on a portable gramophone.

'I remember we were stopped by some German 88s hidden in the Bois de Neudon, and it was not until late afternoon of the twenty-fourth that we reached the crossroads beyond the forest at Petit Clamart – many years later, this was to be famous as the site of an attempted assassination of de Gaulle.

Suddenly from the turret of a tank near us, an arm pointed to the right; an excited face in a scarlet forage cap was shouting something. I looked and way below I could see a tiny Eiffel Tower and an enormous black column of smoke rising from what looked like the Place de la Concorde. Was Paris burning, I wondered?'

Soon we were driving through the suburbs. Huge plane trees in full leaf had been felled across the avenues to hinder the Germans. People appeared from nowhere attracted by the rumble of the trucks and half-tracks, and hundreds of hands cleared the road in a matter of minutes. Later barricades of paving stones melted before us within seconds. By now we were knee deep in flowers, the top of the gear handle floating in a mass of roses and dahlias.

'At Issy les Moulineaux, Leclerc's division had knocked out a German tank lurking in a side street. We were dragged from our car by the excited people and taken to a yard behind the police station. Half-naked bodies had just been discovered; along the wall a strange contraption in asbestos bore tar and finger marks in black. Later I found out that the asbestos had been electrically wired so that prisoners forced against it were burned. A new method of torture to me.'

Last night we came close to the Renault works. Next morning it was hard to get the column into formation because some soldiers had tried telephoning Paris and got through. Now dozens of Parisians were queuing up telephoning Paris. 'We're here! We're coming in!' they were all shouting.

'And what an entry. After crossing the first bridge of the Seine and passing the first Metro station we drove slowly past thousands of people lining the streets. We were kissed and hugged till it hurt. Our scarves and insignia had long since disappeared; we only saved our packs by sitting on them.

'There was some sniping at the Port de St Cloud, but at the

Place de l'Etoile it was heavier. There must have been 20 or 30 diehards on the roofs. American tanks began flowing in. Then a hundred yards away at the Avenue Kleber there was a strange and unexpected sight: Leclerc's soldiers and generals; the German army, Kreigsmarine, Luftwaffe, filing out of the side door of the Hotel Kleber with pathetic little suitcases and kitbags. Troops were holding back the angry crowd. The Germans were murmuring in pidgin French 'Prisoniers de Guerre.' Suddenly instead of trying to lynch them the crowd began to sing the Marseillaise. For us who had been preaching on the BBC that we must hold out and have faith that the enemy would one day be rendered powerless, it was strange to see them there in front of our eyes, not undignified but grey with apprehension and beaten at last.

'Then a big paw fell on my shoulder and nearly dislocated it. It was Hemingway: 'The fighting has stopped in the Tuileries' he said, 'Come on, now we can make the Ritz.' We lumbered off in our heavy van hard on the heels of his nimble Citroen, down the bedecked Rue de Rivoli and up into the Place Vendome. When Hemingway walked in the door, the manager said to him, 'Your trunk is still here.' 'Oh God, I forgot,' said Hemingway. It was full of a lot of his early unpublished writings. To my surprise, Jean Cocteau was there, too, and it was funny to see those two men, so utterly different, greeting each other.'

'The story goes that Hemingway liberated the wine cellar?'

'There wasn't much to drink; anything that there was went very quickly.' 'He also went up and liberated Sylvia Beach on the Rue de L'Odéon and cleared the snipers off her roof. He made Paris his headquarters for a few weeks, and I saw him a few times, but then he went back to America and I never saw him again.'

PETER LENNON 1964

Modern Mayhem 1945 onwards

Rubbish

Came one Annual Adminstrative Inspection early in the 1950's. All at the depot had been drilling and polishing for several weeks in preparation. Everything had been painted white or lined up as appropriate.

Even the dustbins behind the cookhouse had been burnished and polished with Brasso. The inspecting General lifted the lid of one and peered inside and the assembled men were horrified to hear him cry, 'What's this rubbish doing in here?'

STEWART WEST

Snowflakes and Sandcastles

A National Service Memoir

At the time when the forests on the river Raab in Galicia saw the Austrian armies fleeing across the river and when down in Serbia one after the other of the Austrian divisions were taken with their pants down and got the walloping they had long deserved, the Austrian Ministry of War suddenly remembered Švejk. *Why, even he might help to get the Monarchy out of the mess!*

from The Good Soldier Švejk *by* Jaroslav Hašek

1. Snowflakes

I had been in France, working my way as an external student through a course of studies at the Sorbonne; and beginning to research what would become an on-going obsession with the life and times of Cardinal Richelieu. This latter, towards the end of my year, took me to Rouen, the great inland port and provincial capital of Normandy. Also under the wing of a splendid family who introduced me to beef cooked rare, and cut as thinly as smoked salmon. Together with good Burgundy at nearly every meal.

The night before I was scheduled to depart, the family, as a special treat, decided to drive me to Deauville on the coast for a first taste of the Casino circuit. At this moment in time, I should point out, my earthly possessions consisted of a Dieppe-Newhaven one-way ticket, a grip filled with books and well-worn clothes, and about six pounds cash. However: with the six pounds cash I then, at roulette, had the original 'beginners luck'. Beginning with modest gains on the sidelines, *Le Rouge et le Noir,* when I moved to the numbers proper all continued to go well. Later I quit while well ahead, having accumulated what was for me, if not a king's ransom, at least a knight's one. I promptly stood the family a midnight buffet – lobsters were cheaper in those days – and forgot about England for the next four months.

Consequently, when eventually I did re-cross the Channel to submit for National Service I was nearly nineteen and very much under a cloud. But the Army itself also faced a dilemma. It couldn't court-martial me because I wasn't yet actually *in* the Army. At the same time to take civil action risked some bad publicity via the media. *For I had submitted.* In the end, it was decided to let events take their course. I was assigned to the Royal Corps of Signals with basic and trade training at Catterick Camp.

Somewhere near Hammersmith Broadway an elderly crustacean who was once an Army doctor delicately examined my penis for telltale signs of VD. After which, in another office next door, a curry-countenanced Captain who was still Regular Army barked: 'There's no OCTU for you, my lad. YOU'RE LATE!' I explained in the mildest possible terms that I wasn't seeking to become an officer, merely to complete my two years. His complexion changed from Madras to Fal Bangalore. 'Don't bandy words with ME!' he shouted. 'You National Servicemen make me sick! No sense of duty! No patriotism! No interest in Queen and Country!' Then his voice changed gear; down to a menacing growl: 'I expect you're a Socialist as well.' I wasn't, in fact. But I kept quiet. If I'd mentioned being a Francophile and also something of a Bonapartist, admiring the First Consul's energy and promotion on merit, I thought the Fal Bangalore might turn into a major stroke...

Three weeks later, on a train chugging north towards Richmond, I looked out upon the passing countryside with mounting trepidation. Too late I realised having made a far bigger blunder than failing to be punctual. For I was now entering the Army at the end of November, when the beautiful Yorkshire Moors turn extremely inhospitable. There was snow already; and more would fall every day during my five months at Catterick. (Since then I have never needed to go on winter sports' holidays; and the only snow I care for is on Christmas cards.)

This was in 1951. Our barracks for basic-training had been condemned since 1915. Long low buildings of crumbling red brick – as well as broken pipes, so more water ended up on the washroom-floor than escaped into the antiquated sewerage system.

Two previously only heard-of things now became reality. *Bullshit* and *Square-Bashing.* We were not allowed to have a fire in the barrack-room because its two fireplaces were kept permanently blackleaded and polished for morning inspection. That was 'bullshit.' As a result, when we went out to do drills ('square-bashing') our denims, still wet through from previous days of bad-weather drilling would usually freeze to our bodies. Some of us lost patches of skin. Almost as painful as banging the stock of a Lee-Enfield 303 against an innocent and therefore unprepared collarbone. During those first four weeks I had a continuous cold. Death itself would have been considered welcome on certain mornings. And in any case preferable to reporting 'Tom-and-Dick' (sick). For to do that you had to stuff a medium-size pack with all variety of things; and then check all one's remaining kit into the Quartermaster's store – including humping your mattress, bedding and iron-bedstead. All this to discourage malingering. But difficult if you were genuinely ill.

'Did you shave this morning?' the Squadron Sergeant-Major bawled on our initial parade.

'Yes,' I replied, feeling decidedly itchy inside my ill-fitting uniform.

'Yes WHAT!' This delivered as a scream of shock (at my impertinence) mingled with self-righteousness, but above all sheer *rage*.

'Yes, sir!'

'That's more like it!' This delivered only inches from my right ear. With both malice and warning. 'You're an 'orrible little man. WHAT ARE YOU?'

'I'm a horrible man – sir.'

'Good. And now that's understood, *Signalman:* let me give you a piece of advice. When you shave tomorrow morning, TAKE A SHORT SHARP STEP NEARER THE RAZOR!'

One important early lesson to be learned was Never Volunteer. For *anything*. A musician who thought he was in line for a paid Saturday-Night gig with 'Excused Duties' ended up being detailed off to move the piano in the Sergeant's Mess. If one had a light it was better to find a bushel as well. Although at least one member of our intake had given the Army rather a nasty shock (albeit a temporary one). An apprentice chef from The Dorchester, not unnaturally he had volunteered for the Catering Corps. Frightened almost witless at the prospect of unleashing such standards upon the Army's own sacred and infamous institution, the

Selections Officer hurriedly decided he would make a perfect Royal Signals driver.

We were, I suppose – given the benefit of hindsight – a fairly motley crew who met to train and be trained together; and would then go out to defend the tottering Empire. There was the bank clerk with a problem over marching. (His natural inclination was to swing his arms in parallel.) Also the London barrow boy whose parcels from home kept us supplied with little luxuries in the food line – *at a price*. Then there was the lad from Bootle our Corporal ordered to be scrubbed with a yard brush because he was shy of washing himself. And a silent and slightly sinister young man we discovered was an undertaker's assistant. Since I was that bit older than the rest of the intake they always addressed me as 'Dad.'

But the bullshit remained the same for all of us. It wasn't just a matter of boots, brasses and webbing. The day the Orderly Officer found a spent match behind the rifle-rack it was as if the Four Horsemen of the Apocalypse had descended upon us! While every day without fail somebody's bedpack would be hurled out of the window into the mud for not being sufficiently straight or incorrectly folded. Best (or worst) of all though was the monthly business with our bedside chairs. Each of us had one: just an ordinary collapsible wooden chair. To occupy any spare moments left us, in the course of our four weeks' 'basic' we had to razor-blade all the varnish off these chairs. It then became the task of the next intake to re-varnish them – and so on. The chairs themselves meanwhile were gradually getting too thin to sit on. However: in the Army, bullshit stopped for no man. Especially not the National Serviceman. The Regular Cadres held enormous powers. And the Royal Signals being a comparatively young Corps, they felt compelled to catch up on their senior colleagues in the Guards and Line regiments...

Bullshit continued to be the order of the day when we

moved on to trade-training. I can remember one inspection by the Princess Royal (she was the Signals' Honorary Colonel, and feared even by the Corps' own officers). Normally such inspections were a formality. All the real inspecting had been done by senior NCOs before the men go out on parade. But on this particular occasion, after keeping us waiting on the parade-ground for two hours, the said Royal, looking like a faded string bean in BD (battle dress), quite deliberately walked *behind* the drawn-up ranks, pulling back belt-buckles, looking for smears of blanco left on the metal. To the true embarrassment of our officers, many 'fizzers' (charges, resulting in 'jankers': confined-to-barracks, with 'fatigues': heavy physical duties) followed.

On the other hand, trade-training did bring me the first real bonus of National Service. I was selected for Ciphers and Wireless; which involved touch-typing on teleprinters and perforators, which in turn has been of immense value to me throughout the remainder of my working life. I did not have to give out this piece for typing, for instance.

Also too we were allowed out on Saturday Nights. To spend our weekly pay (thirty-eight shillings), or what was left of it after buying blanco and boot-polish, and regular deductions towards a mysterious fund called 'barrack-room damages,' on jam doughnuts, cheap fags and a weak lager at Catterick's NAAFI Centre. If it wasn't one's turn for guard-duty.

Mention of which, but more specifically the Guardroom itself, brings back a last bizarre memory of Catterick. I still think of it, as if from its own Chinese horoscope, as the Night of the Rat.

Although more modern than our basic-training barracks, in the quarters we had moved into for trade-training there was a resident rat underneath the floorboards. It would come up after lights-out via a hole beside one of the radiators, scuttle about and generally become a nuisance just as we were trying to die into sleep. Until the night when some desperate insomniac put his boot over the hole. Only to find in the morning a large chunk of the heel had been gnawed away. Our rodent gourmet evidently liked leather *hors d'oeuvres*.

Clearly special measures were needed now. Beginning with a visit to the Guardroom by three of us and reporting the pest to our Regimental Police.

They were awesome figures, these Regimental policemen; especially their Provost-Sergeant. In the absence of an Orderly Officer he was invested with Jove-like powers, including the deployment as thunderbolts of extremely unpleasant 'fatigues.'

This particular Sergeant, a local Yorkshireman, was well beer-gutted, slow of speech and even slower of thinking. But not so slow that he couldn't catch up with the piece of verbal lunacy about to be perpetrated by one of my two companions. 'Us'll 'ave to contact the Rodent Control Officer,' he said. Then: 'Are yoo sure it were a rat? What did it look like?' To which my idiotic fellow-Signalman replied: 'I dunno. I haven't seen it yet. It's just there. But I'm sure it hasn't got any stripes up!' And that was it. All three of us spent the next nights 'bumpering' (polishing) the Guardroom-floor. Meanwhile the rat itself had survived another intake.

2. Sandcastles

'Very well then, Švejk,' said the Lieutenant in a solemn voice. 'I wish to tell you that you are going with me on the *marsbatak* (march battalion), if you like such abbreviations. But don't think that at the front you'll be able to drop such bloody awful clangers as you've done here. Are you happy?'

'Humbly report, sir, I'm awfully happy,' replied the good soldier Svejk. 'It'll be really marvellous when we both fall dead together for His Imperial Majesty and the Royal Family...'

A sandcastle, according to the dictionary I use most frequently, is 'a mass of sand moulded into a castle-like shape, esp. made by a child on the seashore.' Add that what can appear both imposing and complex is easily swept away by the tide of events and you have some idea of the British presence in Egypt in the early 1950s.

At 'the crack of sparrow-fart' (or 5.00 a.m. to be precise) I was roughly awakened in the gloom of a World War II air-raid shelter beneath Goodge Street Underground station and summoned to a breakfast of 'shirt lifters' (baked beans: subsequently renamed 'blazing saddles' since Mel Brooks' film) and tinned, skinless sausages. My Army service in foreign parts was about to begin.

By that night I was in Malta, with overnight accommodation in a large, airy barracks built centuries before by the Knights of St. John (still more comfortable than Catterick). The following midday I was at El Adem, in the Libyan desert: a desolate airstrip with only its flyblown NAAFI and half-a-million jerrycans for orchestration. Then the next morning I reached the Canal Zone, behind its multiple barbed wire one of the longest armed camps since Passchendale and the Somme. It would become, for me, the start of a personal relationship with Egypt (or Egg-wipe as certain old sweats insisted on calling it) which in several ways is still going on. For the moment though, the Army had merely transported me there.

It was also an important time in Egyptian history. King Farouk, in a last, desperate attempt to stave off the coming revolution by focussing his people's wrath elsewhere, had unleashed a small, unpleasant guerilla war against the British encampments between Port Said and Port Suez. For too many years his own ruling activities had consisted of high stakes at Monte Carlo, devouring half the Shah of Iran's caviar exports and cruising Cairo's street at night in the Royal limousine to pull in and rape young girls – whose families

were then threatened if they protested. Meanwhile the ordinary *fellaheen* starved. So now, while young officers led by Nasser and Sadat plotted his overthrow with General Neguib, the King's chosen commandos indulged in a so-called 'popular' dirty tricks campaign; which included stretching thin wires across the Canal Zone road at night to decapitate our motorcycle riders. It ended when the British lost patience and shot up the Egyptian police-station in Ismailia. When Farouk's fate was sealed, the people wanted to string him up, Mussolini-style from the nearest streetlight; but Nasser saved his life and packed him off into exile.

However, when I arrived much of this was still in the immediate future. On my first day all I noted in my diary was changing from BD into cotton-drill and being jeered at as a 'nig-nog' because my knees weren't brown. Plus yet another medical inspection. As we lined up one of our number suddenly developed an enormous erection. I never did discover whether he fancied the MO. But he was immediately put on a fizzer 'for showing dumb insolence'.

We were assigned to small marquees with stone paved floors and 'boxes-soldier' (tin trunks for our kit). Also a bedside cabinet. Six Signalmen to each marquee. The tents were dangerously tinder-dry, and that same afternoon one was hit by a swirling dust-devil and lifted fifty feet in the air, guy-ropes and all. It fell back to earth (sand) looking like a crumpled elephant. Another kind of guy, with the bed opposite mine, had decorated his bedside cabinet with an ornate *ER1.* It turned out he was a Scottish Nationalist. This 'affront' to Queen and Country went undetected through all officers' inspections over the next eighteen months. Whereas on only my second parade I got pulled up for not having the right number of studs on the underside of one of my boots. Obviously even under war conditions bullshit still reigned. (Not long after this a grizzled veteran of El Alamein told me how, in the early morning light before the second battle, one of Monty's officers had held a cigarette-lighter under each man's chin to make sure he'd shaved!)

Actually my own particular coming work for the Army was soon to spare me much of this bull; but in that first, settling-in week I wrote home 'it's just like Catterick with sun.' Came the weekend though and my new Scottish friend conducted me along the Canal Zone road, past the bustling *souk,* over the Sweet Water Canal with its inevitable quota of dead dogs and on to the evening's entertainment at our area cinema. On the way, passing the local shops, he threw a piece of wood at what appeared to be a bunch of grapes hanging up. In fact it was a hunk of meat swarming with bluebottles. The cinema was open-air; and I commented on the big front-gates lying off their hinges. Yes, my friend explained: the previous week they'd shown a Marilyn Monroe film, and when the 'House Full' sign had gone up a large overspill crowd had rioted and stormed the entrance. The troops were so starved of sex they even wolf-whistled the Queen at the end of the programme.

There were at this time approximately 90,000 British Army and RAF personnel along or near the Canal Zone – a majority beside the Great Bitter Lake where De Lessops' link between the Mediterranean with the Red Sea is at its widest. There were perhaps 1,500 females (including NAAFI staff). Any WRAC with neat ankles, a compact bum and shimmering breasts could command her own equivalent of a Troubadours' court. Even the plainest had her followers. The village brothel near where I was stationed at Fayid remained strictly out of bounds. With most of us scared off in any case by the lurid films of syphilitic ravages we'd been forced to sit through in England. Although I do rememeber two Irishmen chancing their luck one night. Surprised in the middle of it by the Military Police, they pulled up their trousers and ran out of the building the back way, took a wrong turn in the dark and ended up in the Sweet Water Canal. Then subsequently in a British Military Hospital having their stomachs pumped out. Before being put on special fizzers (Commanding Officer's Orders).

But to return to the military and political situation in Egypt. Apart from our land troubles with His Royal Gluttony, King Farouk, GHQ Signals at Fayid had become Britain's 'key' overseas communications centre. There were the Gloucesters and other contingents fighting under a United Nations' flag in Korea. There was the on-going 'War of the Running Dogs' in Malaya; and the Mau Mau rebellion in Kenya. Plus rumblings of EOKA in Cyprus, a threatened Left Wing insurrection in Jordan (we had a radio station at Aqaba, and another in the north at Mafraq) – and a weird situation under the aged King Idris in Libya, where our link (from Benghazi) was morse-code only and run by Greek civilians. Almost every piece of military information and political evaluation from these various operating spheres had to be relayed to the War Office in London via our powerful SSB transmitter in the Canal Zone. (SSB: Single Side Band, allowing up to eight teleprinters or perforator-heads to transmit different messages in parallel over the same frequency.) We took messages in from everywhere, even Malta and Hong Kong; and we passed them on, given the eccentricities of the ionosphere.

Imagine my consternation, therefore, when I first fell off a dilapidated World War II truck only to discover that the vital 'nerve centre' of our fading Empire around the globe consisted of two long, rusting Nissen huts with a cockroach-infested 'brewing up' cubicle in between. Consternation turned to something worse as, that same night, being a trained operator, I was put on the direct link to War Office, London. For, what I had to operate *with* was a clapped-out, pensioned-off, ex-Post Office teleprinter! With, beside me, a perforator-head which took the greatest delight in chewing up 'Operational Immediate' tapes which had taken hours to prepare. The busiest man on our shift was the maintenance technician (Thank God a very well-trained Regular, of full Corporal rank). Every night he was kept – to quote my friend Quincy Jones of someone else – 'as busy as a one-armed paperhanger with lice!'

At 9.30 p.m., while still struggling somewhere in the deep-end to the 'War House' (I've always loved Evelyn Waugh's description of this Holy-of-Holies, nowadays for political reasons renamed the Ministry of Defence), and endeavouring to patch together yet another broken tape of two thousand or more encoded groups about a fresh enemy offensive in Korea, I felt a brisk tap on the shoulder. I looked up. I couldn't believe it! My Shift Supervisor and even my new Colonel were there, the former rigid, both pale-faced. The man who had tapped my shoulder was none other than General Robertson (he who later tried to run British Rail; alas!), the GOC Canal Zone. 'Get that routine stuff off the airwaves, Signalman.' He spoke with condescension, but not unkindly. 'And send this first. O-pip' (meaning Operational Immediate). 'And stand up and salute the GOC', one of his ADCs shouted at me. 'But I can't salute, sir,' I replied, by this time grown canny regarding Army rules and regulations, 'I haven't got a hat on.' The young ADC in his highly-polished Sam Browne flushed darkly – but clearly had made a slip. 'Stand to attention then,' he ordered – with markedly less confidence. 'But, sir,' I pointed out, 'I can't send this *urgent* message standing up.' General Robertson smiled, wanly; and motioned for me to proceed. He was not exactly the most charismatic of men. I read his message. I hand-typed it through. Received the acknowledgment. The Top Brass retired. It was a birthday greeting to one of his relatives. Afterwards I began to pick up the pieces of the semi-destroyed tape about the Gloucesters' casualty-list in Korea...

Several months later General Robertson was replaced by the best senior officer I was to encounter in the British Army, General Sir Cameron Nicholson. And it coincided with my beginning to be promoted towards Shift Supervisor. This General understood communications, obtained better equipment for us and most evenings would wander across from his office just to find out for himself if all was well. Over the same period, in moving up to the supervisor's desk, I gained from another intake fresh out of Blighty a black-haired (crew cut), short, scrawny Birmingham-born signalman with a marvellous twisted smile called Bennie Lynch. He was the finest natural keyboard operator I've ever met in my life. If he isn't in the higher echelons of IBM or Cable and Wireless today then there's no justice. I locked him into the War House circuit immediately. And then felt free to sort out various problems on the link circuits. Most notably with our two civilian operators on the troubled Benghazi link, Christadoulou and Solomonides. They were brilliant operators, but temperamental and they spent half their time day-dreaming about Cyprus. Eventually Solomonides quit and went back to Nicosia. He preferred driving a taxi to the morse-code and said in any case it paid better . . .

We worked a regulation 3-day shift system. An afternoon from one o'clock to six on the first day. Then the 'crusher' on the second: a morning from eight till one and an all-nighter (fourteen hours) from six to eight. The third day we had off. During most of which we sought a sleep of the dead underneath our mosquito-nets. Most of the time things worked well. Except when during the long night-shift the ionosphere decided to go up the spout and we had to change frequency. Real trouble. And it nearly always happened if there was an EMERGENCY telex from General Sir Gerald Templer in Malaya to relay on. Fortunately he was a most succinct communicator. He could lambast the War House in a very few words. For which our operators and myself in relaying his cipher were extremely grateful.

But if things had started to go well for me at GHQ, they were proving far from easy at the Signals' regimental base camp. An old and repellent form of Squadron Sergeant-Major had turned up there, ironically with a Gallic-sounding surname, promptly to be nicknamed 'Froggy.' He was large, loudmouthed and a malicious rumour went round that he'd been in the Army eleven years before gaining his first stripe. He was also very bullshit. On his first Pay Parade every man in the Squadron was ordered to wear his shorts longer and his hair shorter. Whereupon some unseen wag at the end of the line had called out, 'Get yer knees brown, yer nig!' The authority in question whirled about, then, failing to spot the culprit, ordered the six men nearest to him to go on fatigues. Clearly the battle lines had been drawn.

In theory Froggy had little or no control over my movements because my job with the Army was now considered of strategic importance. Also I had the sympathetic ear of our own Regimental Sergeant-Major (who really ran the whole show at base camp). Provided I continued to clear the log jams of messages at GHQ I remained reasonably beyond Froggy's reach and excused all purely squadron duties.

Except that I had to keep my tent 'immaculate'; and off-duty to behave at all times 'with good conduct and military discipline.'

Even so, 'the swine's definitely out to get me,' I complained bitterly to Bennie Lynch and another operator, Duffy, over our bottles of Stella, the local Egyptian beer. 'He resents not being able to order me around. And worse still, as an old-style Regular he hates the fact of a National Serviceman having been promoted.' My friend John Knight agreed. John occupied the unenviable position of Squadron-Office Clerk and had to put up with Froggy all day long. 'Yes. You're certainly on his hit-list,' he said. 'The man's a menace. He even drinks his mid-morning mug of tea by numbers. But as operators you should all be okay over the next few weeks at least. There's a General's Inspection coming up and he'll be too busy supervising the bullshit to further any personal vendettas.' I signalled Abdullah the waiter to bring us another round of Stellas.

Actually the General's Inspection proved a general disaster for Froggy. It was discovered that some person or persons had been doing unspeakable things into the fire buckets. Also the sole of an OR's boot had dropped off in the middle of the barrack-square parade. Worst of all though: in order to get one up over the other squadrons, our zealous SSM had ordered the sparse grass outside his office to be blancoed a brighter shade of green. And then wondered why it proceeded to wither and die before the appointed day. The inspection earned him a CO's reprimand. Which did little to improve his relations with the remainder of the sqaudron.

My own bad relations with him came to a head several weeks later. By this time I'd begun to write music scripts and broadcast them over BFBS (the British Forces Broadcasting Service). Where one day Neville Powley, Programmes Controller for the station, asked me to share the compering chores with him at a 'live' jazz concert at RAF Shalufa. To do this meant swapping shifts with another NCO Supervisor. Whereupon Froggy jumped at the fact that I hadn't obtained his permission. Hauled up in front of him, I stood my ground. If he took the matter further, I threatened (adding a respectful 'sir'), I would put in an offical request to the CO for transfer to BFBS on a fulltime basis. Froggy wavered; and then backed down – reducing his voice to half its usual level of decibels. He knew the regiment didn't have a spare Shift Supervisor at this moment in time. He would earn another reprimand for bringing about the situation. *However*, mine might just as easily prove to be a Pyrric victory. For, as John Knight confirmed that same evening over our Stellas, not only was I on Froggy's hit-list. I was now Public Enemy Number one.

The conflict continued; coming to a climax of meanness with the arrival of Christmas (in itself a contradiction in terms, since Christmas in Egypt is warm and sunny). Froggy, with normally no control over my movements, discovered I had five days off from GHQ Signals – and promptly inked me in for Regimental Guard Commander on Christmas Day itself: a 24 hour duty. Thoroughly pissed off at the prospect, nevertheless I decided to take no chances. Exactly a month before, on the prowl as usual, he had caught the whole Guard House asleep, stolen in, silently removed their rifles, then 'called out the guard' – to their total bewilderment, being half-asleep and without weapons – and charged every man of them. The Sergeant Guard Commander was busted down to Signalman. (And if Froggy ever got me back as a Signalman... I shuddered at the prospect!) So I resolved to remain *on guard,* literally. Even if it meant no sleep for the whole 24 hours.

In fact it proved to be a fairly spectacular Christmas Day, and Night. Whether good or bad depends on one's personal viewpoint, of course.

Froggy and one of his few friends (toady/sycophant) got

well and truly plastered in the course of the morning. Whereupon they decided to give the long-suffering Other Ranks a Christmastide treat. Adding a sponge soaked with gall and vinegar transposed from Good Friday to the glorious so called Rest Day. (Oh! If the Egyptians had attacked 3 GHQ Signals that same morning, they could have had a walkover!) Wearing a striped *djellaba* and donning a bright red *tarboosh,* the SSM's burly figure approached the ORs' lines over the loose, sandy football pitch, followed by his dwarfish minion. They lined up all the fire buckets, took a stirrup pump and proceeded to spray the ORs' tents: Froggy's friend, by this time almost legless, holding the nozzle. Where it all fell apart for them, someone (my own mucker Duffy was later both accused and congratulated, but kept strictly silent) crept up behind the junior Sergeant – and gently eased him around. The harder Froggy pumped, the more he got back. And, we presumed, it was still somewhat infused...

After a slipshod inspection on the barrack-square by an equally-befuddled Orderly Officer (another 'nig' Second Lieutenant just out from Blighty) I took over officially as Guard Commander at 6 o'clock that evening. Despite the temptation of several bottles of good Cypriot brandy in the tent (a Christmas present from Christadoulou), I had managed to stay strictly sober during the day. Also, I knew Froggy was likely to be sober again and on the warpath with a thick head by this time. The situation reminded me of the protracted duel between Mr Flay and the fat cook, Swelter, in Mervyn Peake's Gothic novel, *Titus Groan.* Only in this case Froggy would not be leaving 'an exquisitely sculpted gateau' first as his visiting card. Given the opportunity, he would be coming directly at me with his cleaver.

I was beginning to enjoy the Army work now; as well as writing and broadcasting scripts for BFBS; and I didn't want to be busted. So I took the utmost care with everything:

including posting every sentry myself, although I had a Lance Corporal as Deputy.

But as it turned out Froggy was totally excluded from the final dramatic events of that night.

Around midnight an out-of-breath and ashen-faced barman arrived from the Officers' Mess: separated from the Sergeants' and ORs' areas inside another barbed wire compound. (Generals fight from the rear these days and generally die in their beds.) Much military mayhem had broken out over there. The CO was away. The still-befuddled Orderly Officer had lost control of his seniors. He had been grabbed, his hat turned back-to-front and they had all danced *Ring-A-Ring-O'Roses* about him. But now there had been a serious accident...

I woke the Lance Corporal. Told him to take over the guardroom and log-book. Woke an off-duty signalman. Stuck his rifle in his hands. Picked up my Sten. Then we headed for the Officers' Mess.

After much heavy drinking, and having disposed of the Orderly Officer, a number of them had climbed out onto the flat roof of the two-storey building – *and started drilling.* Until the officer calling the commands forgot to give the about-turn. When the front four went over the edge. I arrived to find two with broken legs and one with a broken arm and collar-bone. Only their drunkenness had saved them from further damage; perhaps even broken necks.

It wasn't easy to find a working switchboard at midnight on Christmas Night, anywhere along the Canal Zone. Still less to persuade a British Military Hospital six miles down the Canal Zone road that I wasn't joking and would they please send an ambulance. Urgently!

When our CO returned the following morning, Boxing Day, the whole of the Officers' Mess was Confined-to-Barracks (plus double duties) for a month. I was summoned and thanked for my promptitude. And that lunchtime, in the

Sergeants' Mess, the RSM really rubbed it in. Speaking to Froggy directly, but also to everyone else within earshot, he said: 'Horricks behaved just like a Regular, didn't he?'

Froggy made no comment. Grimly, he downed the rest of his beer and returned to his own Squadron Office. Only to be confronted by John Knight, his Clerk. Holding at arm's length a very large piece of cardboard. 'Excuse me, sir. But I found this pinned up alongside Squadron Orders. The lettering has been done with something very nasty.'

Froggy took it from him and pulled a face. 'Yes. I can smell it!' Then he read aloud 'CLANGERS WILL NOT BE DROPPED, INSTEAD THEY ARE TO BE HIGHLY BULLED AND GENTLY LOWERED TO THE GROUND.'

...I thought about Tolstoy and what a great advantage an experience of war was to a writer. It was one of the major subjects and certainly one of the hardest to write truly of, and those writers who had not seen it were always very jealous and tried to make it seem unimportant, or abnormal, or a disease as a subject, while really, it was just something quite irreplacable that they had missed.

from The Green Hills of Africa *by* Ernest Hemingway

Again, if this memoir had been a full-length book, instead of an insert inside another full-length book, it would have needed to have everything in it. Especially about Egypt itself. About how beautiful the dawns were; purple, then deep cerise and – finally – a very light pink before the sun would let any of the day through. And about the way the night itself would fall with the speed of a zip-fastener, when *immediately* all the stars were visible in the sky. (You had to be on guard-duty to appreciate these things properly.) Also about the desert itself. Trillions upon billions of grains, now serene, now shifting about to cover over the dirt of Man. Patient too, like a great material God. No matter what follies the human animal perpetrates across it, the desert is real and it remains. Only Man (including many British and Egyptians) and the creatures and colonies of ants progress towards death. Deserts do not die.

By comparison with these tremendous existences, the sun, the sky and the desert, any other details in my portrait must seem small; even petty. But they were there at the time, and I have room for a few more of them...

I remember the needle-sharp points of those shells on the bed of the Great Bitter Lake. If one didn't swim, it was just the same as treading on well-laid barbed wire. And I can remember perspiration hardening on my face in the cool of the evening so that it felt like a coating of gum. Also the shrewdness and laughter of the Egyptians who operated our *dhobi,* pounding the British uniforms into tatters against the inside of an enormous metal drum. With always Cairo Radio buzzing out Arab 'pop' songs in the background. (It was these same *dhobi wallahs* who gave me the free 'run down', not too greatly exaggerated, on Farouk's procured sex-life. My God! How the ordinary Egyptians hated him.) But what an amazing complex of relativities the human process of memory is! Now I can see all those scratched and battered Egyptian buses hurtling along the Canal Zone road as though driven by religious fanatics who see the Islamic paradise straight ahead – or feel the hot breath of many devils behind. *Such buses:* the wheels pointed in the right direction, but the chassis appeared about to lunge off the road. And the outside was always obscured by the brown faces and billowing robes of non-paying passengers. (At least, no Egyptians ever gets left at a bus-stop!) However, we had been on foot that day when I saw the bloated, maggot-covered camel floating in the Sweet Water Canal – only a hundred yards down from where children were paddling and Egyptians using the water to make coffee. I think it was the same day too that I saw the family dying of *bilharzia;* with the puddles of their blood-stained urine all around the house. And yet, I know that before the Sweet Water there had been no crops at all in the area. Yes; I who averted my sensitive nostrils whenever the shit-wagon drove past. I who had overcome my moral aversion to opium, and found the smoking a pleasant experience; who liked the hot taste of *arak* just as much as the taste of whisky. But I couldn't stand the smell of an ordinary shit-wagon, which Egyptian labourers toiled on every day. And before the wagon came we had to dig deep pits for the stuff.

Which poses another question. Why was the only man in the regiment allowed to catch VD off a lavatory-seat the padre?

And now, for no particular reason I am reminded of Egyptian trains: stripped of everything by the passengers except for the woodwork and wheels. And the level-crossings: just two lengths of chain draped across the road, and a signpost in Arabic and English saying, 'Beware of Trains.' One of the level-crossing keepers was the only Egyptian boy I ever met with blue eyes. He told me his father had been an Italian.

Or perhaps I should be writing about the gallows the Army built, out in the desert. It was to hang a soldier who had gunned down his officer. (The officer had stolen his girl.) But I would prefer not to...

Then there were the good officers. The ones who knew how to lead as well as giving orders. These officers were easy to obey, and we from the RSM down trusted their judgement. However – there were other officers. Establishment figures who never once sensed the mood or thoughts of the soldiers under them. Like the Brigadier who ordered a 17-mile night march across the desert in full kit. The perspiration soaked through my shirt and into my pack and saturated every single thing in the pack. At the end of the march we waded far out into the lake – still fully dressed – hoping to cool our burning limbs and smouldering boots. Officers over the age of forty had been excused the march. The Brigadier who ordered it was forty-five.

If I made this portrait complete it would say a lot about my exhilaration during that particular shift when I found I could 'take' messages as fast as London could send them. But also how much alcohol I drank when off-duty. And it would have to include some mention of the Nissen hut I discovered which contained 5,000 books, and where I could read Baudelaire and Rimbaud and Gerard de Nerval. Also, how the Church of England/Church of Scotland kept us supplied with new books and British newspapers and many little comforts from home, while my own Catholic Church supplied only its orders to attend Mass.

It would describe, too, other parts of the Middle East. Cyprus, for instance. And being on detachment in Jordan, where two operators collapsed because they forgot to take their salt tablets. And what a fine country Jordan was scenically; with a fine people and a courageous young king.

And the flies and the flies and the flies. (This phrase owes nothing to the Gertrude Stein-stutter, but everything to the abundance of flies.)

Ultimately, despite everything, the British Army was an experience I'm now glad I collected. Within it I grew from a mere knowledge of men and history from books to being a man in a living part of history.

RAYMOND HORRICKS

Indonesian Confrontation

In the mid-1960s Indonesia confronted Malaysia along their borders with Sarawak and Sabah. A small boat called the *Sumpitan* was chartered to carry an initial cargo of urgent supplies, including those for the NAAFI, from Singapore to Labuan which was to be the initial offloading point.

The *Sumpitan* was a ramshackle little boat of about 200 tonnes. The Chinese crew worked reasonably quickly. Crates of every conceivable commodity were hoisted aboard and the Bills of Lading were given little attention. Morale being given a high priority, NAAFI supplies were supposed to be loaded last so that they could be first off.

At last the ship set sail with four British officers, including myself, aboard, and after two or three uneventful days arrived at Labuan together with the torrential rain of the monsoon season. By the time the boat moored alongside Labuan's only jetty we British officers on board were drenched to the skin, cold and thoroughly miserable.

The first person to greet us was the NAAFI manager, also very wet and cold, who promptly asked if his stores could be offloaded first. Together with the small administrative staff on Labuan, we were in desperate need of a drink and were only to pleased to comply with his request.

In a very short time and still in the pouring rain five or six crates were loaded onto the jetty and were duly carried up to the go-down (warehouse). Eager hands set to work to get at the bottles of whisky which the NAAFI manager assured us were in them.

The first crate was finally opened. The manager winced and so did we. It contained nothing but Tampax.

Feverishly we set to work on the second crate and then the third. They all contained Tampax. By this time the ears of some 'Q' Staff Officer in Singapore must have been red hot. The NAAFI manager was crying tears of frustration and tempers were running short.

At long last we found what we were looking for and had something to warm us up. Our spirits improved immediately, though it must have been a strange sight in that go-down, four officers and the NAAFI manager drowning their sorrows with neat whisky and surrounded by hundreds of boxes of Tampax. Someone in Singapore had certainly got the loading sequence wrong, especially as there was only one woman on the island and she was the nurse.

Warmer now, we moved our brains into action. What could we do with such a cargo? One very bright officer, who merited a promotion on the spot, had a brilliant idea. The boxes of Tampax were delivered in quantity to the Dyaks who formed part of the British force. Not being acquainted with these items, they took them to be rifle pull-throughs and from then onward the cleanliness of their barrels was the envy of all.

MAJOR R.M. BREWER

from *'A Message from the Falklands'*

HMS GLAMORGAN, 22 May 1983 [received, 10 June]

Your long marvellous letter of 6 May arrived today via *HMS Leeds Castle* (a most inappropriate name for a ship!) which is acting as postman between us and Ascension Island. It was like a breath of sanity coming into this totally mad world here. I am glad that you think that way about Mrs Thatcher and the war – as I have come to think since this business started. I sometimes wonder if I am totally odd in that I utterly oppose all this killing that is going on over a flag. Wilfred Owen wrote that 'There'll come a day when men make war on death for lives, not men for flags', but it has been the reverse here – 'nations trek from progress' still.

It is quite easy to see how the war has come about; Mrs Thatcher imagined she was Churchill defying Hitler, and the Navy advised a quick war before the winter set in; the Navy chiefs also wanted maximum use made of the Navy for maximum publicity to reverse the Navy cuts: which has happened. For [utmost] worth, victory or defeat would have the same result; publicity and popular support, either congratulations or sympathy. The Navy thus overlooked the fact that we were fighting without all the necessary air cover which is provided by the USA in the Atlantic and by the RAF in the North Sea and Icelandic Sea. Although the Harrier is a marvellous little aircraft it is not a proper strike aircraft, and the best the Navy could get when carriers were 'abolished.' Consequently, we have no proper carriers which can launch early-warning aircraft fitted with radar as strike aircraft. From the Fifties onwards these two were absolute essentials.

However, the Navy felt that we were British and they [the Argentinians] were wogs, and that would make all the difference. The Admiral said as much to us on [the task force] TV. Consequently, we have no way of spotting low level attacks beyond 20 miles, which is how *Sheffield* was sunk. In a grandiose statement after the *Sheffield* loss, Nott stated that the Nimrod aircraft (early warning) and more Seawolf Type 22 frigates (which can shoot down Exocet) would be sent to the Falklands to counter the situation. Total lies! There is only one more Type 22 frigate and Nimrods have not appeared – even if fitted with in-flight refuelling gear it would be a difficult job for them. The only way we can counter these missiles is to keep out of range, which is what we have to do.

Apart from the military fiasco the political side is even more disgraceful. Even if Britain does reconquer the

Falklands we still have to talk to the Argentinians and come to some arrangement, so why not settle before a war has devastated the Falklanders' island? However, if Britain is going to turn the Falklands into a garrison island (in direct contravention of the Antarctic treaty?) it will show the complete hypocrisy of the British government which was going to leave the islands totally undefended and take away the islanders' British citizenship! I suppose Mrs Thatcher will have to let them become British again – if so, will we provide them with a proper British health service, money for development, etc.? The garrison alone, with married quarters, NAAFI, hospital, barracks, air base, naval base, repair facilities, etc., bringing in, say, 3,000 people at the minimum (including dependants) will have to be taken out of NATO – so more defence spending when the RN is to be cut by a third! Or, maybe, not cut the RN after all this publicity, and increase defence spending by, say, a third. The forces will have an immense millstone around their necks; people will not want to go there (going to Scotland is hated enough) and the NCOs and Senior Ratings will simply leave the forces. The whole business is absolute nonsense.

I read that Argentina was prepared to accept a deal which involved Argentinian sovereignty and British administration and way of life. Those, to me, sound fair terms to avoid bloodshed. Now that war has started, neither side can give way until the other is exhausted. This is not a war between civilised countries. It is not fought for any good reason (trade, survival, top-nation status etc.) but is fought on a 'principle' by two dictatorships. It is a dangerous state of affairs in Britain when the Prime Minister can tell the forces to go to war without consulting even Parliament. If that is the case, it is time the forces were cut so that it is impossible to use them for anything but the defence of Britain, and [that] they were placed under NATO control. Thinking of wars fought on 'principle' alone I can only think of religious wars of bigotry, and the Thirty Years War which destroyed Germany. Thinking of enormous expenditure, I can only think of the Spanish Armada, the Dutch Wars of Independence – and Suez! A classicist on board also quoted an example of another dying power having a last fling. I only hope that the Falklands do not become our Vietnam, but so long as this government is in power they will be... Mrs Thatcher, and our Admiral (he, more understandably) seem to have no compunction about casualties at all – the initial shock of *Sheffield* has worn off, and now they are accepted willingly – 20 yesterday in a helicopter, and 20 in *Ardent*. And they will not end until one side surrenders.

DAVID TINKER, LIEUT, RN

Epilogue

The late Robert Capa was, in the opinion of this book's editor, the greatest war photographer of all time. It was the opinion of Ernest Hemingway too; and of John Steinbeck, who said: 'Capa's pictures were made in his brain – the camera only completed them.'

His first published photograph was of Trotsky preaching war in Copenhagen in 1931. Subsequently he covered the Spanish Civil War (where the love of his life, Gerda Taro, was accidentally crushed to death by a tank), the Sino-Japanese conflict and the whole timescale of World War II. He took the finest pictures of the D-Day landings. All eight of them. He gambled his life going in with the first wave, only to lose the rest of his pictures – ninety-eight – at the hands of a slipshod darkroom assistant.

He photographed again in Israel in 1948, and in 1954 was in a bug-ridden room at Nam Dinh preparing to cover the war in French Indo-China. He could not lose his fascination. 'This is going to be a beautiful story,' he said. 'Maybe the last good war.' Two days later he took a mortar-shell full in the chest. He died with no knowledge of what would become of Vietnam.

All wars, large or small, right or wrong, are horrifying. And still they go on.

> 'No weekends for the gods now. Wars
> Flicker, earth licks its open sores,
> Fresh breakage, fresh promotions, chance
> Assassinations, no advance.
> Only man thinning out his kind
> Sounds through the Sabbath noon, the blind
> Swipe of the pruner and his knife
> Busy about the tree of life...'

(Robert Lowell)

But while warfare is horrifying, it is frequently accompanied by idiocies, ironies and above all, mayhem. Many battles have been fought to a conclusion despite the presence of mayhem – *often committed by the desperately lucky victors!* At a distance and/or given the passage of time, the humour in the mayhem becomes obvious; and as such this book can be treated as an entertainment. Nevertheless it has its undercurrent of seriousness too. An intended reminder that, while we are entitled to laugh at some of those goings-on in the military life, it is a monstrous pity that Mankind cannot uproot the whole need for militarism from his inner nature. Alas, there is as yet no sign of it...

RAYMOND HORRICKS

CODA

This story is somewhat apocryphal, and almost certainly polished up over the years – although a former Grenadier Guards officer assures me it is true. It comes from the early part of World War II, when the German Panzers swung around the Maginot Line at great pace and smashed the British Expeditionary Force and the French Army. Hitler could be very pragmatic when it suited him. He had promoted a brilliant, young and also partly-Jewish colonel from the German Staff College, Erich Von Manstein, to general and adopted his plan to push the Panzers, spearheaded by General Guderian, through the forests of the Ardennes; previously thought impossible to penetrate with armour. As it was happening an English general, who shall remain nameless, refused to believe what was going on, and, instead of preparing himself and his troops, took himself off for a swim. When he returned from his dip, still dripping and with a towel about his waist, it was to find General Guderian sitting at his desk...

RAYMOND HORRICKS